Clacton-on-Sea
in old picture postcards

by
T.A. Baker

European Library - Zaltbommel/Netherlands MCMLXXXIV

Cover picture:
This is the famous 'Koh-i-Nor' and this photograph may be of her arriving at Clacton on her maiden voyage, in 1892, and this view of the Pier must be that year since the Pavilion on the end was begun towards the end of it. Both this vessel and the 'Royal Sovereign' were built by Fairfield & Co., Glasgow, the latter vessel coming into service a year after 'Koh-i-Nor'. For many years they were the largest vessels of their kind in the London excursion services. The 'Koh-i-Nor' was 310 feet in length, had a beam of 32 feet, and a speed of 19½ knots. Both vessels were able to sail from Old Swan Pier (above London Bridge) because they had telescopic funnels and hinged masts. The Paddle Steamer 'Jupiter' saw one of these Palace Steamers go under the bridge and thought that she could do the same, thereby smashing both her funnels. The 'Koh-i-Nor' and 'Royal Sovereign' were built originally for the Victoria Steamship Association. They were taken over by the New Palace Steamship Coy. in April, 1895. If this is the maiden voyage of 'Koh-i-Nor', she was shortly due to suffer an unfortunate experience, for on the run back to London a canvas awning over her fore-deck was set alight by sparks from the funnels. The decking caught alight as well, but eventually the fire was put out. Mr. W. Houghton gives an account of this incident: 'I was a passenger in 'Koh-i-Nor', on her maiden voyage (to Clacton) during which her deck boards caught light going home. The 'Clacton Belle' stood by us up to Tilbury where we all had to leave her and go on to Fenchurch St. by rail...' Despite this mishap she survived to become one of the most popular paddle steamers on the London/Clacton run until 1903 when she was transferred to the Dover service.

GB ISBN 90 288 2776 5

European Library in Zaltbommel/Netherlands publishes among other things the following series:

IN OLD PICTURE POSTCARDS *is a series of books which sets out to show what a particular place looked like and what life was like in Victorian and Edwardian times. A book about virtually every town in the United Kingdom is to be published in this series. By the end of this year about 175 different volumes will have appeared. 1,250 books have already been published devoted to the Netherlands with the title* **In oude ansichten.** *In Germany, Austria and Switzerland 500, 60 and 15 books have been published as* **In alten Ansichten;** *in France by the name* **En cartes postales anciennes** *and in Belgium as* **En cartes postales anciennes** *and/or* **In oude prentkaarten** *150 respectively 400 volumes have been published.*

For further particulars about published or forthcoming books, apply to your bookseller or direct to the publisher.

This edition has been printed and bound by Grafisch Bedrijf De Steigerpoort in Zaltbommel/Netherlands.

INTRODUCTION

Clacton was really the brain child of a brilliant and inventive engineer named Peter Schuyler Bruff, who had worked on the local railways on the line up to Ipswich and also the Tendring Hundred Railway. He had a love of the calm peace and golden sands of Clacton beaches – there was no village nearer than Great Clacton and the surrounding countryside was all farm land and trees. The willow trees grew in such abundance along Holland Marshes that the Hawk Moth flourished in great numbers.

It was also an ancient pre-historic site, for about five hundred thousand years ago, in an inter-glacial period, the River Thames flowed this way and one of its loops can be traced from Lion Point, Jaywick to the beach below Tower Road. In the cliffs and along the line of the loop have been found the remains of 'Elephas Antiquus', Woolly Rhinoceros, Sabre-toothed Tiger and a large deer to which was given the name 'Dama Clactoniana'. The oldest known wooden artifact in the world, the fire hardened point of a broken spear, was discovered by Hazzeldine Warren, an Essex Archaeologist, when CUDC workmen were digging into the cliffs to build a shelter below Nelson and Tower Roads in 1911. He also discovered an early flint flake industry, now known to archaeologists throughout the world as the 'Clactonian Flint Flake Industry', and the whole period is known as the 'Clactonian Era'.

Long after these first residents on our shores had gone, moved on by the last recorded Ice-age, and the North Sea had flooded the course of the old river, there is evidence of 'New Stone-Age' man with traces of their primitive huts and crudely decorated pottery known as 'Rinyo-Clacton' ware.

About the turn of this century, the 'Clacton hoard' of ancient gold coins was uncovered, probably by a cliff fall, these were of the period of the Belgic migration. They date from circa 90 to 70 B.C., and are known as 'Clacton Type'.

There are signs of Roman occupation too; a small hoard of fourth century copper coins minted at Trier in the reign of Constantine the Great (A.D. 307-337) was unearthed on a building site near Holland haven, in those days an estuary where ships might shelter, and Roman bricks and tiles are incorporated into the fabric of St. John's Church at Great Clacton.

Coming to more modern times Peter Bruff obtained the interest of the Woolwich Steam Packet Co. to his idea of building a Pier, etc. The reason was simple; they had for many years run a successful service to Margate on the Kent Coast. Margate was about 70 miles from London by sea, and they thought a stopping place about the same distance along the Essex Coast would add to their existing service up to Harwich and Ipswich. Bruff discussed his scheme to build a Pier at Clacton with William Parry Jackson, chairman of the Woolwich Steam Packet Co., in the summer of 1870 whilst walking along Clacton beaches. Jackson agreed to the scheme and arranged for their steamers to stop at the Pier when it was built. Peter Schuyler Bruff had acquired the cliff lands at the sale in 1865 of the estate by Mr. J.Y. Watson (known for his book 'The Tendring Hundred in Olden Times'), but it was not until 1871 that the Pier got built and Clacton-on-Sea began to emerge as a reality.

The Royal Hotel was built and the first houses went up in Rosemary Lane in 1872. Gradually the place grew and in 1877, in what is now Pier Avenue, the Public Hall with its adjoining assembly rooms, library and reading rooms was built. About this time it was noted that 'Extensive Improvements have been made... Handsome residences have sprung up in all directions, and the town, as viewed from the Pier, now presents a general outline of the plan originally laid down by the promoters of the undertaking'.

By Bruff's far sighted planning, and his 'Deed of Mutual Covenants' which laid down certain standards with regard to buildings etc., which had to be observed, a fine, well laid out town developed. Indeed, it may be claimed for Clacton that it was one of the first towns to benefit from Town Planning. A railway extension from Thorpe was completed in 1882, and from thence onwards there was intensive rivalry between the G.E.R. and the various Steamboat companies which began to run excursion services to Clacton.

During the 1890's the town grew rapidly, and by 1895 Clacton Urban District Council had come into existence: the fleet of 'Belle Steamers' were running; big hotels such as the 'Towers' (1891) and the 'Grand' (1897) were built and most of the central town roads were made up. By the end of the century the first Motorised Public Transport was running. In 1901/02 the row of shops known as Electric Parade was built and opened and, indeed, the early years of the twentieth century up to the First World War were a period of frenetic activity, with all sorts of schemes being developed such as the 'Reno' Electric Stairway up the cliffs; the 'Palace by the Sea'; and many others.

The town became a national focal point when the great combined Naval and Military Manoeuvres in 1904 took place. H.R.H. Field Marshal the Duke of Connaught, Inspector General of the Army, acted as umpire-in-chief, and Edgar Wallace, then a journalist, dubbed the proceedings 'the Invasion of Letspretendia'.

From the early days when buildings were more important to the embryo town the story of its development gradually gave way to people. People of all sorts; those who came to the town on excursions; those who were an influence on its development, those who braved storm and tempest in its lifeboat service and those who were entertainers. Then there were the great and the famous who visited the town for one reason or another. All left their mark great or small and this volume is an attempt, not at being a History – this has been admirably done by Kenneth Walker in his excellent 'History of Clacton' – but a pictorial record of the town's development by photographs taken by witnesses to the contemporary scene.

Acknowledgements:

I would like to acknowledge with grateful thanks the assistance given by the following:

Essex County Library and Mr. S. Sullivan, A.L.A., Group Librarian, Tendring area, for permission to use many of the photographs and postcards in the Local History department of Clacton Central Library.

Mr. S. Cornish, A.L.A., and the staff of Clacton Central Library.

Mr. K. Walker, for his invaluable help and permission to quote from his definitive 'History of Clacton'.

Councillor Laurie King, for his local knowledge.

Doctor P. Tooley, M.Sc., Ph.D., for advice on the text.

Mr. G. Hardwick for information on Great Clacton.

Colonel John Cramphorn, photographs of 1904 Manoeuvres.

Mr. I.F. Trinder, to quote from his book 'The RNLI and the Masonic Lifeboats'.

Mr. D. Johnson, photographs of Passmore Edwards Home and Cars at the 1904 Manoeuvres.

Mr. V. Gray, Essex County Archivist.

Mrs. K. Baker, for help with the typing.

Tendring District Council.

Mr. D.R. Geale.

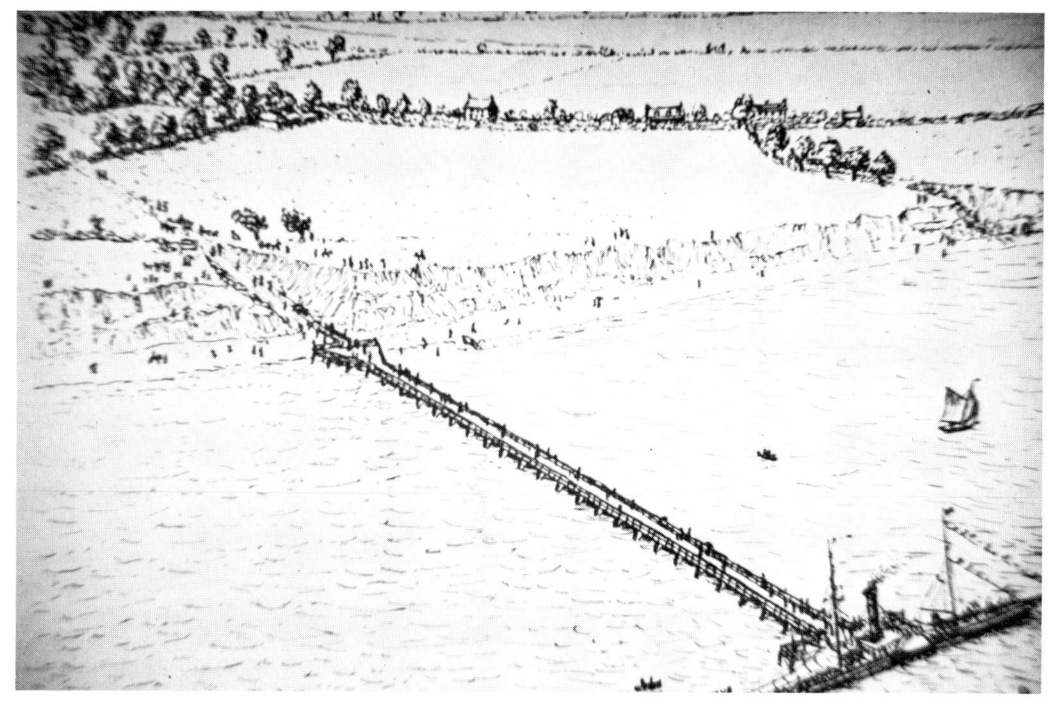

1. THE BEGINNING OF CLACTON-ON-SEA. Clacton-on-Sea owes its origin to *An enterprising gentleman, Mr. Bruff, who... determined to convert this spot into a watering place, and being seconded in his efforts by the Woolwich Steam Packet Company... succeeded in the early part of the present year in erecting a Pier as the preliminary towards the object he had in view...* ('The Times' – 31st July, 1871.) This drawing by Kenneth Walker, shows the first Paddle Steamer to berth at the Pier, on 18th July, 1871. Next year, in 1872, the 'Royal Hotel' was built just behind the two trees at the top of the Gap. The Pier was lengthened about seven years later. Peter Schuyler Bruff, son of a Trafalgar sailorman, was a brilliant engineer. He has a road named after him in present-day Clacton.

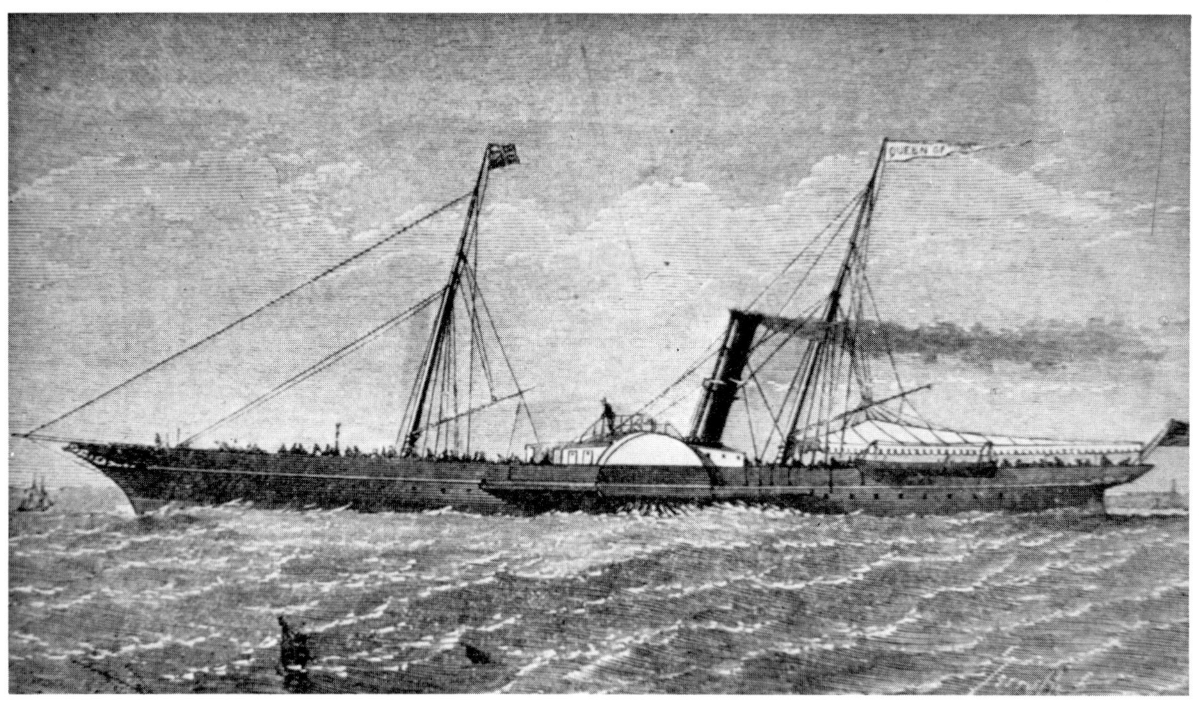

2. 'QUEEN OF THE ORWELL'. With the flag on her after-mast proudly announcing that she is the 'Queen of the Orwell' this is the vessel which carried William Parry Jackson, chairman of the Woolwich Steam Packet Coy., and a party of guests to visit the new Pier at 'Clacton Beaches'. The trip was repeated just over a week later on Thursday, 27th July, 1871 by the saloon steamer 'Albert Edward', with Mr. Jackson and nearly 300 guests on board. They left London at 9.30 a.m., arriving at Clacton at 2.45 p.m. The plans for the future town were discussed. *...a few semi-detached villas, hotels and boarding-houses, open spaces for recreation and promenades along the cliff. Clacton-on-Sea has this great advantage, that being entirely a new creation... none of the evils inseparable from old watering-places will be allowed to exist in it. There will be no slums, nor any object that can offend the eye...* ('The Times' – 31st July, 1871.)

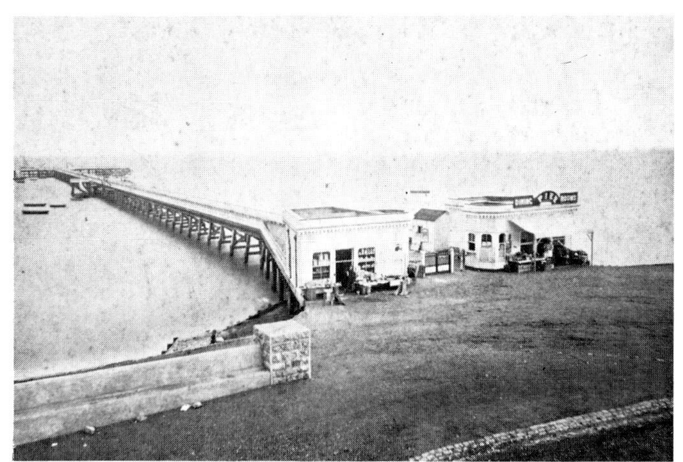

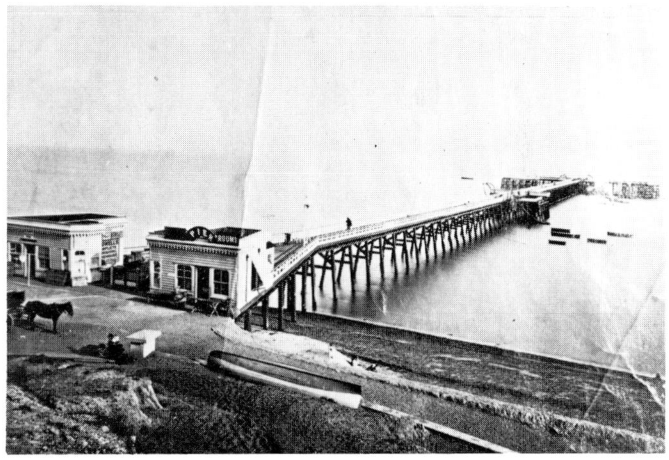

3. FIRST PHOTOS OF THE PIER. Early photographs of the Pier as it was a hundred years ago. The sea wall, which can be seen on the first picture, was built in 1881. The 'Pier Dining Rooms' and the other building were both leased by Mr. Wallis, proprietor of the 'Royal Hotel' in 1885 and turned into 'Hot and Cold Sea Water Baths'. The second photograph was taken after the word 'Dining' had been removed, and a pair of davits added half way along the Pier. The building on the left of the Pier entrance carries a notice – 'Powells complete furnishing warehouse'. A scale of charges was laid down for sea-borne cargo. A barrel of Gunpowder was charged at 6d. Musical Instruments: 1d. per cubic foot. A corpse: £1. Since the passenger fare from London was only 4/6d or 5/- you were, to the Pier Authority, worth more dead than alive. These are interesting, as they are the earliest known photographs of the Pier, and date from between 1881 and 1885.

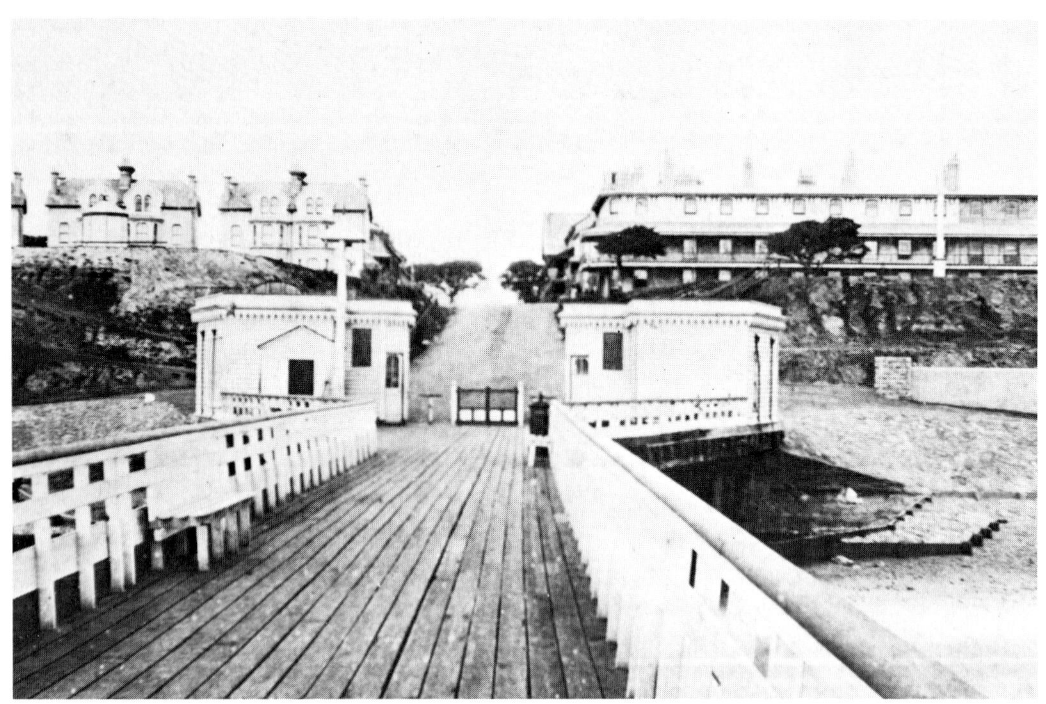

4. LOOKING UP PIER GAP. Looking from the Pier up Pier Gap. The Royal Hotel is top right and the two trees shown in picture No. 1., can be seen in front of it. Also on the right is part of the sea wall, built in 1881, which extended as far as Vista Road. Here the Pier Gap road is unmade and there are no shops along either side of the Gap, these came in 1887. So this picture dates from between 1881 and 1887. The original Pier, seen here, was quite narrow, only about 12 feet wide. An order was applied for in 1888 to enable it to be widened and in 1890 this work was carried out. Note the trees in the centre background where Pier Avenue is now.

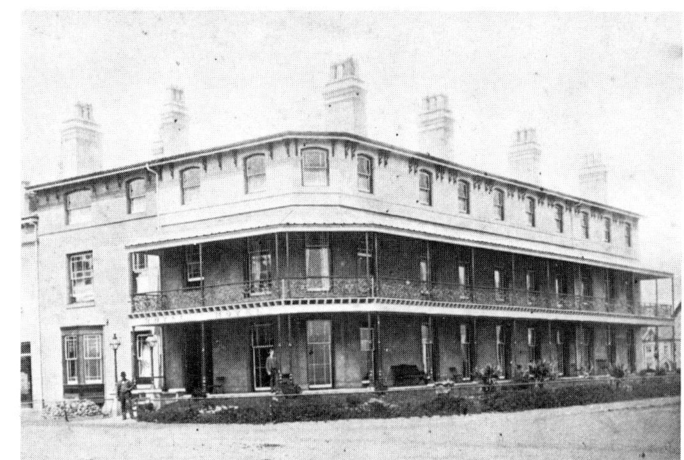

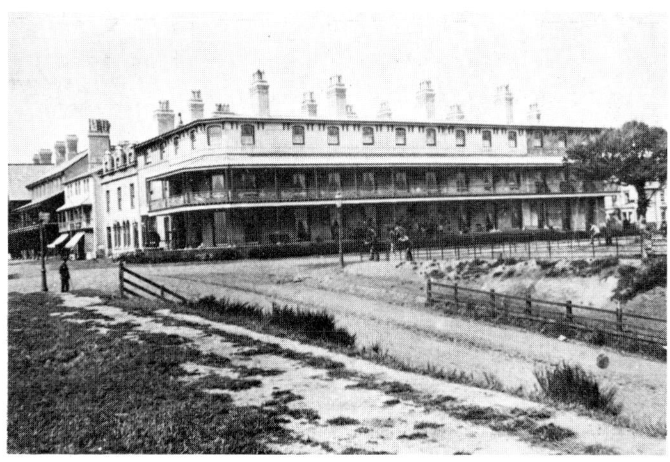

5. THE ROYAL HOTEL, CLACTON-ON-SEA. The Royal Hotel celebrated its Centenary twelve years ago, for it was opened on 24th July, 1872. It was built at the top of the Pier Gap. At its opening, the Chairman of the Hotel Company modestly stated that 'It would no doubt prove satisfactory to those visitors who desire to exile themselves from society of every description...' A somewhat gloomy and certainly less than optimistic assessment, but, after all, when built it was only surrounded by fields, and there were no roads, only a muddy gap down to a short Pier. But as holidays became increasingly important to all classes, the new Town, which began its existence by a fortunate coincidence in the same year that Bank Holidays were legalised, thrived and grew. Twenty-six years after it was opened, the 'Royal' was used by H.R.H. The Duke of Connaught, Queen Victoria's third son, as his H.Q., during Military exercises on the Coast. The first photo is earlier, pre-1881, for in that year an extension was built which can clearly be seen on the right in the second.

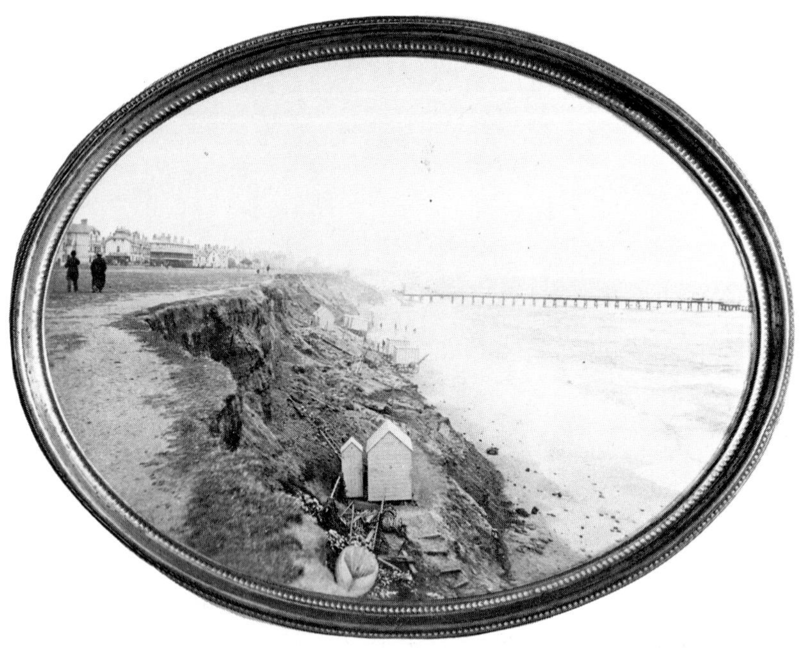

6. FOUL WEATHER AND CLIFF FALL. An intriguing photograph taken during a severe storm. Note the heavy surf and big waves. Quite considerable damage has been caused to the cliffs, cliff paths and bathing machines. It may be the occasion when, in 1883, the Battery and its guns, sited in front of the Martello Tower about 400 yards West of the Pier, fell down the cliffs due to erosion. Certainly there has been a considerable cliff slide. The bathing machines have been drawn up the beach as far as they can go and there are a number of men 'beach-combing'. After storms like this many interesting things are washed up or uncovered. The 'Clacton Hoard' of Gallo-Belgic gold coins came to light in this fashion in the early years of this century and individual gold coins continued to be recovered right up until the 1930's. Skeletons, bones and teeth of 'Elephas Antiquus' and other pre-historic animals, such as the Woolly Rhinoceros, Sabre-toothed Tiger and a type of deer given the name 'Dama Clactoniana', have also been uncovered. Incidentally the guns which fell down the cliff in 1883 remained in the sand until 1905 when they were dug up and mounted on gun carriages in Anglefield to celebrate the Centenary of the Battle of Trafalgar and death of Nelson, in 1805. They were removed during the First World War and doubtless went for salvage.

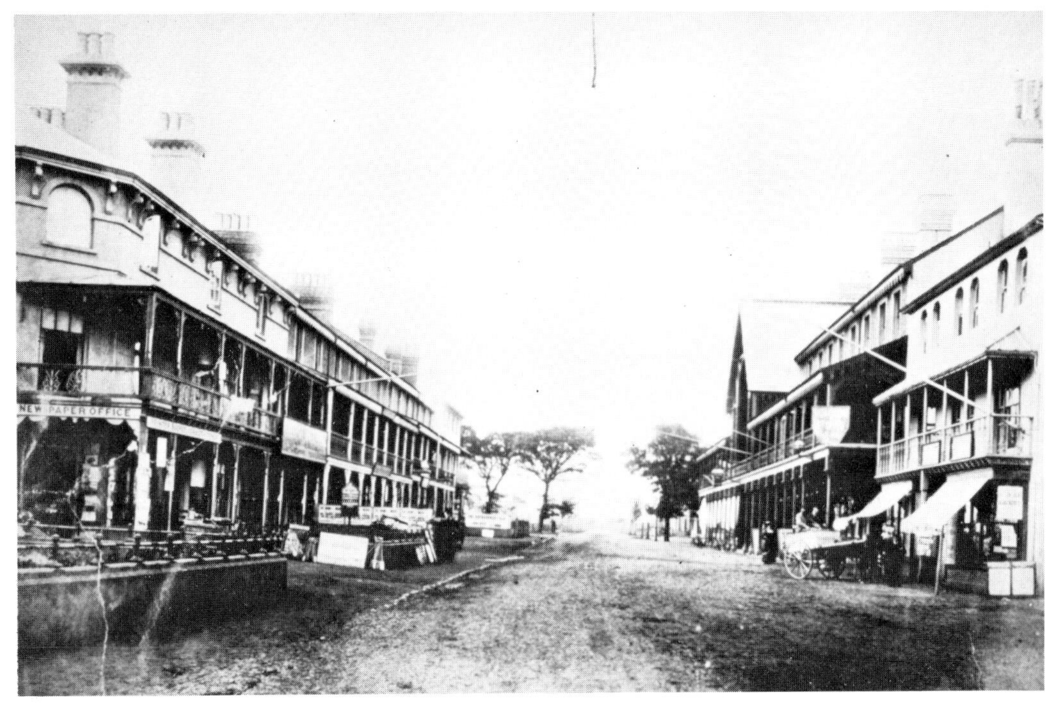

7. A WILD WEST TOWN. The view up Pier Avenue a hundred years ago. On the right there is the Public Hall with its adjoining assembly rooms, library, reading and retiring rooms and shops opened in 1877. The first pair of houses on the left, originally known as 'Clarence Villas', were built as private residences in 1876. Later they were converted into The Clarence Restaurant, and a newspaper office as seen. There are few buildings beyond what is now the junction with Pallister Road, and the trees on the left mark the future West Avenue. To complete the appearance of a 'Wild West' Town, the muddy unmade road appears to stretch out to nowhere; it is now the heart of the shopping centre of Pier Avenue. Although there are few buildings beyond the junction, small trees have been planted to mark the road. The date is 1879 or the early 1880's. Pier Avenue was made up in 1891.

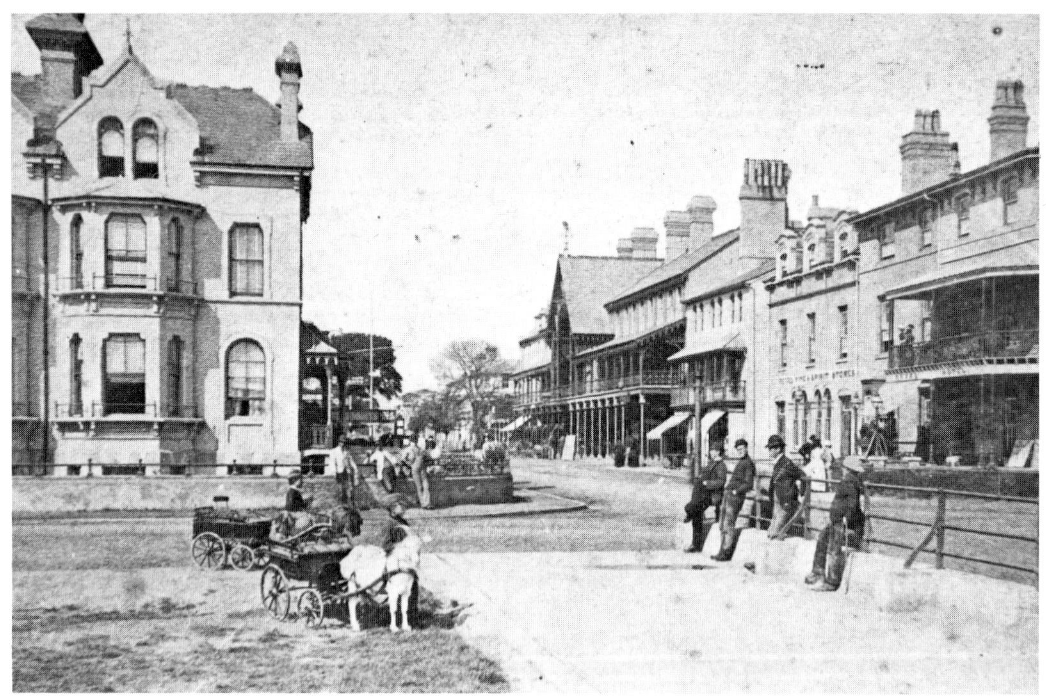

8. PIER AVENUE, EARLY VIEW. A view showing more clearly the Public Hall and Assembly rooms with the colonnaded arcade, middle right. This later became Lewellen's Stores until it was destroyed in a disastrous fire just before the beginning of the Second World War. It was built in 1877 and for sixteen years was the focal point for much of the Town's social life, being in frequent use for concerts, dances, meetings, etc., then it was incorporated into the adjoining shop (Lewellen's) whilst the Assembly rooms became the home of the Clacton Club. This photograph was probably taken in the early 1890's. A concrete path has been put down abutting Pier Gap and there are more shops in Pier Avenue. The left foreground shows a white goat harnessed to a cart to give children rides for 2d. Just behind is a pony cart. A number of workmen are taking their ease: perhaps it is lunch time.

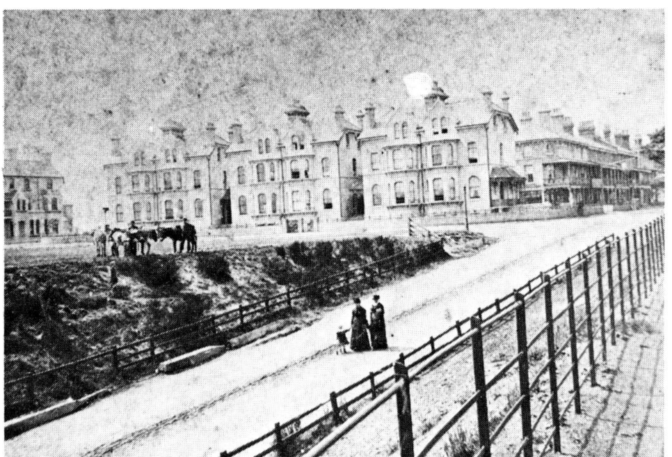

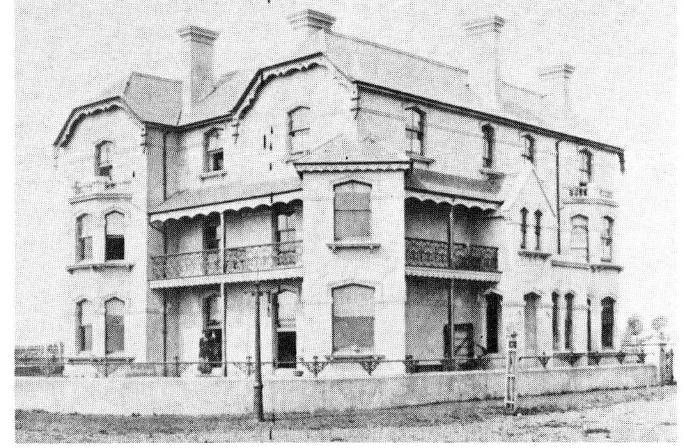

9. Above: THE 'BLOCKHOUSES'. In 1874 these three pairs of houses were built along Marine Parade West at a total cost of £3,000 which was a considerable sum in those days. They were named 'Anglesea Villas', but got nicknamed 'The Blockhouses' by irreverent Clactonians of those days. It can be seen that the roads are still unmade but a gas-lamp has been installed at the top of Pier Gap. There must have been other holiday visitors around apart from the two ladies and young child going down Pier Gap for there are three or four donkeys available to give pleasure rides (left). The sea wall west of the Pier up to Tower Road was piled in March/May 1889 and officially completed in October 1889, so if the piles to be seen along the left of Pier Gap were being used for that purpose, the date of this photograph would be 1889. The 'College' is on the extreme left.

Below: THE COLLEGE. A seaside school had many attractions during late Victorian times and so it was that as the town grew, a number of small private schools were opened. The first was established very early on, in 1871, by F.J. Nunn at Verandah Lodge in Rosemary Lane. He then moved to Brunswick House in Pier Avenue (later the Brunswick Hotel and now Marshalls Amusement Arcade). This boys school, opened by Messrs. Nunn and Crouch, was known as 'The College' and was built circa 1881. The road verges were being marked out at this time by planting carefully protected saplings. There is also a standard for a gas-lamp which has not yet been fitted. The building is now the Waverley Hotel.

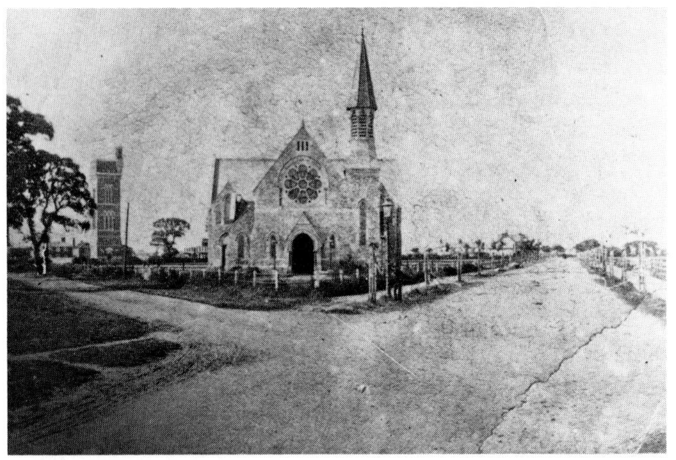

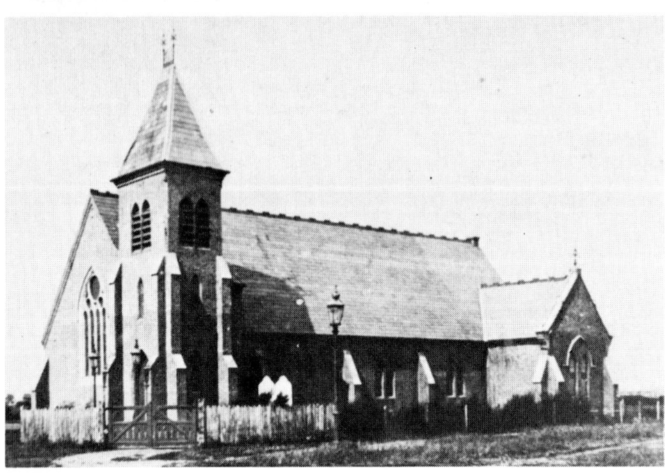

10. Above: TRINITY WESLEYAN CHURCH. Trinity Wesleyan Church, seen here, was built in 1877 and the Water Tower, to the left, in 1881. The road is Pier Avenue with Rosemary Road branching off to the left and joining Old Road where the Water Tower is situated. The roads are unmade and there are no kerb stones, but trees all carefully protected by wooden palings, have been planted on the verges of the footpaths. Pier Avenue continues up into the distance where it joins Old Road, but there are no buildings yet on either side of it. The Church School Hall, which was built in 1887, is not shown in this picture, so it can be dated as being taken not long after the Water Tower was built in 1881.

Below: ST. PAUL'S CHURCH. In August, 1874, a tender of £883 was accepted for the building of a new Church on a plot of land given by H.J. Page, of Thorrowgood Farm. He was selling off plots of land eastwards of Carnarvon Road up to Victoria Gap, below Victoria Road. Later in that year the Foundation Stone for the new Church was laid by James Round, M.P. Seven years later, in 1881, the Church was enlarged. The extension can be seen on the right of this photograph. (The roof slates show up lighter where the new extension joins the original building.) The new St. Paul's Church was built on the same site in 1965.

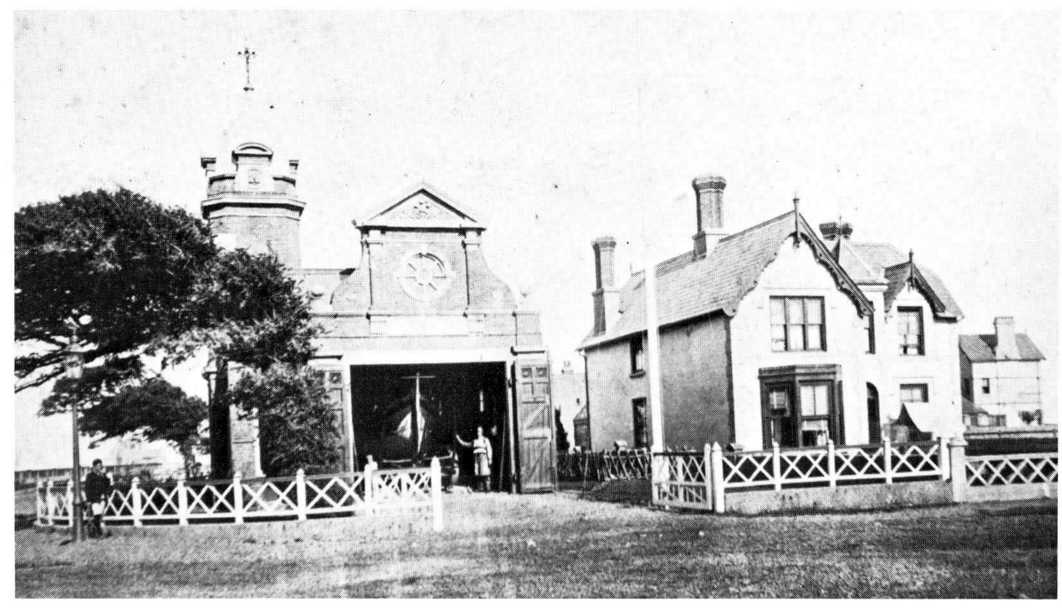

11. THE LIFEBOAT HOUSE. The Lifeboat House and Hadleigh Villa at the corner of Church and Carnarvon Roads near Eagle Gap. The Lifeboat was drawn on its carriage by two horses down Eagle Gap and launched from the shore: a hazardous task in an on-shore gale with a heavy sea running. The Boathouse, designed by C.H. Cooke and built in 1877-78 was enclosed by a fence to protect it from damage by cattle. The round dormer window admitted light to the roof space which housed two large hooks for raising and lowering the boat onto its carriage. A winding staircase led up the tower to the left where a warning bell was hung to summon the crew when needed. *The late Mr. George Hole, who occupied premises opposite the boathouse, related from memory how, in the days of the horse-drawn lifeboat carriage and fire engine, a bell was used to sound the warning from each establishment. Both bells were of different character and tone, and the same horses (used principally for farm work) were employed for both establishments. On hearing the bell they would make their own way to the correct spot and there await their respective crews...* (The R.N.L.I. and the Masonic Lifeboats – I.F. Trinder.) There was an inscription above the doorway: 'This Boathouse Establishment was Presented to the R.N.L.I. and Endowed in Perpetuity by the United Grand Lodge of Free-Masons of England, in Commemoration of the Safe Return from India of the Most Worshipful the Grand Master, H.R.H. Albert Edward Prince of Wales. 1877. Charles H. Cooke, Hon Architect.'

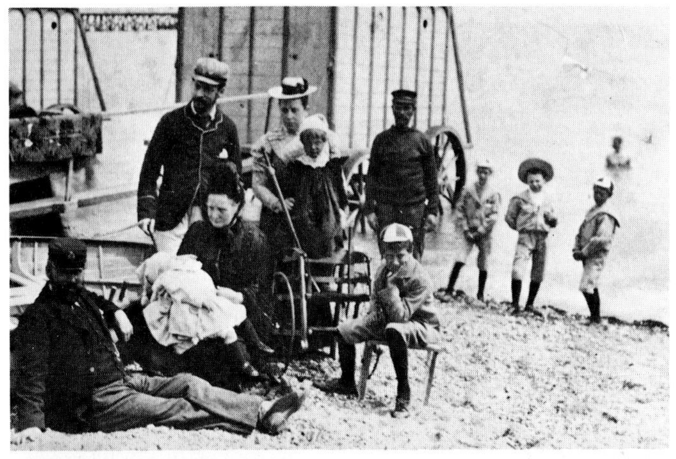

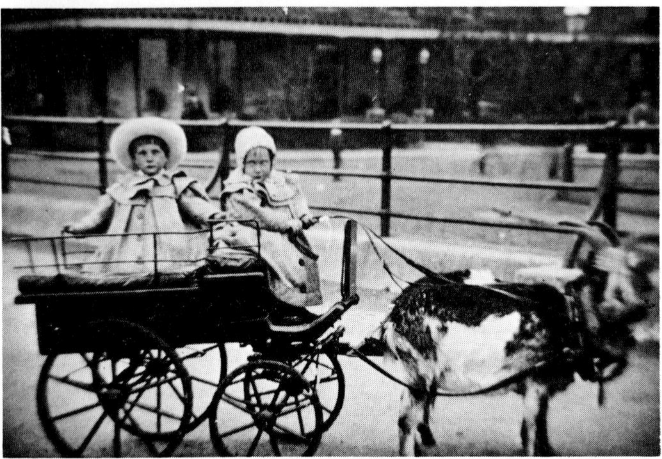

12. Above: THE DRUITT COLLECTION. In 1894 a gentleman named Theodore Druitt took his family to Clacton for their summer holidays. They stayed at 'Erin Villa', Edith Road owned by Mr. & Mrs. Kingsford. Mr. Druitt was a keen amateur photographer and took his big box camera to record the holiday. Eighty years later one of the family, Miss Madge Druitt, who just remembers the holiday – she was two or three at the time – sent the collection to Clacton Library. This family group shows Mr. Druitt, sitting on the sands, Madge Druitt, being held on top of her push-chair, and her four brothers, Russell and Norman by the water's edge, wearing school caps, Reginald (on stool) and Clifford, on Grandma's lap. Harold Hinton, wearing a round hat and standing between the two Druitt boys by the water's edge, was a friend. Notice the formal dress, even for a frolic on the beach. Long shorts cover stockings up above the knees.

Below: A RIDE IN A GOAT-CART. This is another photograph taken by Mr. Theodore Druitt of a typical Victorian sea-side childrens' amusement, a ride in a Goat-Cart. This is similar to the one shown in photo No. 8, but has two Goats harnessed to a central pole. These are Mr. Druitt's two youngest children, Madge at the back, with Master Clifford holding the reins. Madge was about three at the time, and her brother was a year younger. Over eighty years later, she told me this was one of the incidents in the holiday that she did remember, because she had to keep still, and the Goats wouldn't! And the ride cost 2d. The picture was taken on the concrete path at the top of Pier Gap, with the Royal Hotel on the opposite side of the road. It gives a splendid idea of young childrens' dress in the 1890's.

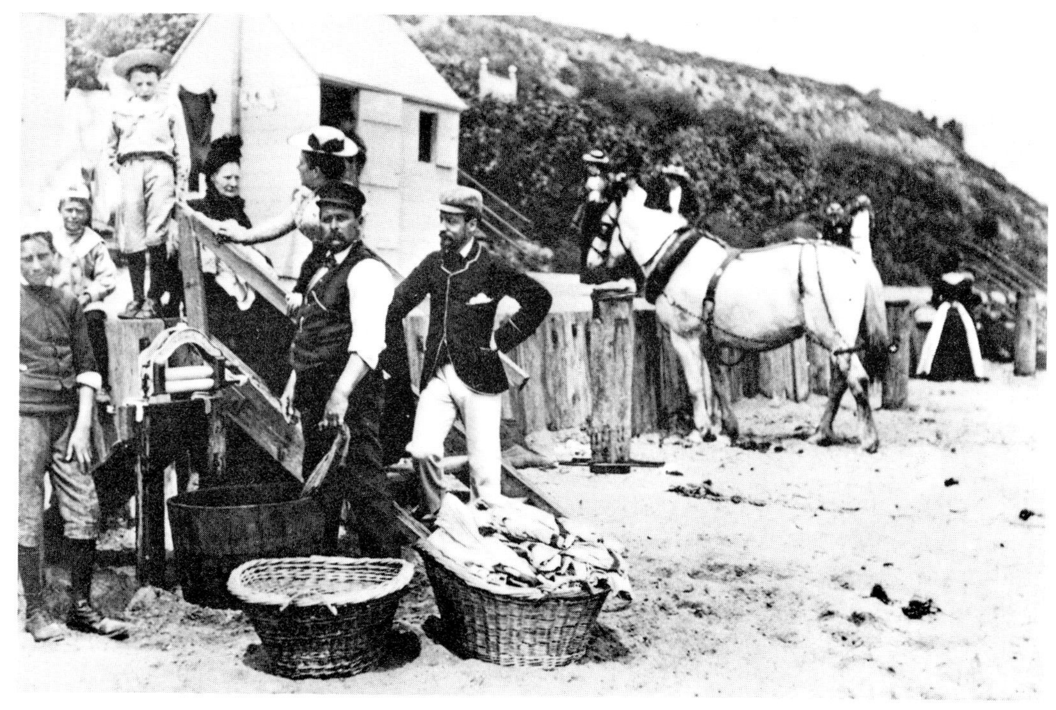

13. WASHING THE BATHING COSTUMES. Another Druitt photograph with a splendid amount of period detail. In those days, if you wanted to bathe in the sea, you hired not only a bathing machine but also a bathing costume. After your bathe you handed the costume back; it was then washed, put through the mangle and hung up to dry and air. The photograph shows it all clearly: wash-tub, mangle, and basket full of bathing costumes. The horse was used to pull the bathing machines down the beach to the low water line, and as the tide came in they were winched up by ropes attached to post winches, two of which can be seen, one either side of the horse. The chap by the wash tub is Mr. A. Cattermole, who owned and operated most of the bathing machines.

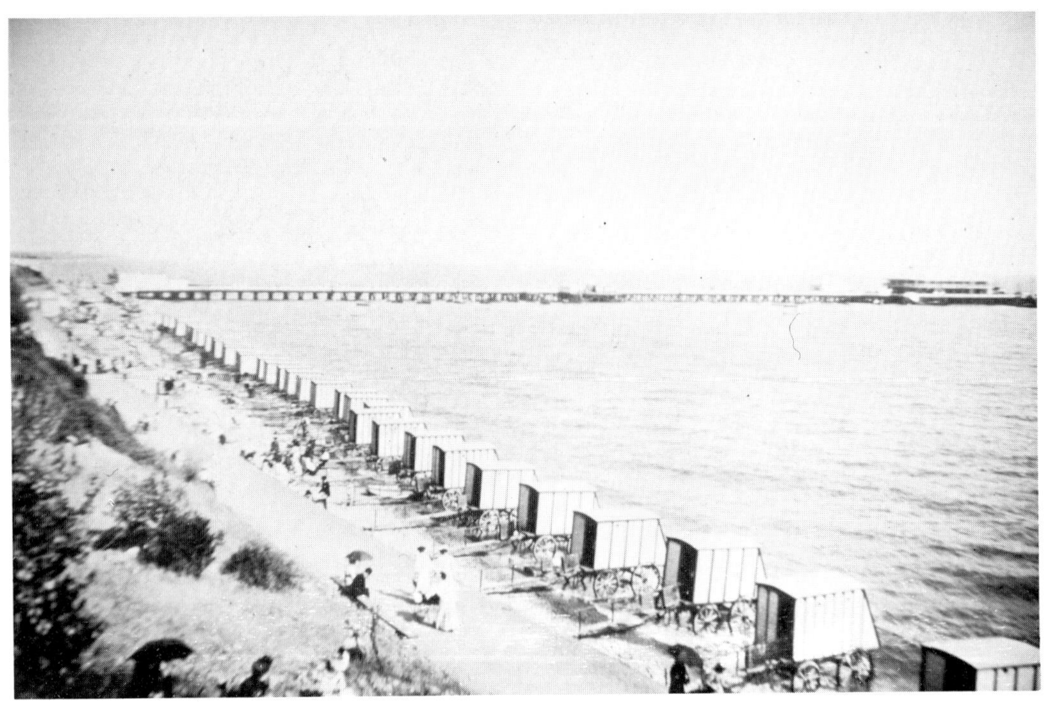

14. PARADE OF THE BATHING MACHINES. West Beach, Clacton, in all its Edwardian glory, at high tide, on a glorious Summers' day, with a calm sea. Each bathing machine has a gang-plank with a hand-rail, so that the bathers can enter, change and then step out of the seaward end into the briny for their bathe. At the Pierhead on the extreme right of the picture can be seen the Pavilion, which was built in 1893, but this photograph, judging by the ladies dresses, is Edwardian.

15. CLACTON'S FIRST COX'N – THE LEGENDARY LEGERTON. Robert Legerton was made Cox'n of the Town's first lifeboat, the 'Albert Edward', in 1878. The slipways on either side of the Pier were provided in 1886 from a legacy left by Miss Bedford. The boat was then kept on the Pier during the winter being launched down either slipway instead of from the beach. In the course of sixty-four service calls in his thirteen years as Cox'n, Robert had some hair-raising experiences, the worst of which occurred at mid-night on January 23rd, 1884 when, in mountainous seas, after she had set out to answer distress signals the lifeboat was hit by two tremendous waves, and capsized. Two men were lost but the rest managed to cling on: 'the Cox'n was swept right under the lifeboat as it went over and the experience he never forgot, nor did he care to remember it...' For 'Outstanding meritorious Service' he received the RNLI silver medal to which were subsequently added three clasps. Among other awards, the French gave him a Gold medal for saving the crew of sixteen from the lugger 'Madeleine', on 23rd October 1881. Robert's last service call ten years later was both hard and eerie. He took the lifeboat out in a blizzard to the schooner 'J.W. Bebell' aground on the Gunfleet Sands. When he got to her only one mast was visible. In the rigging clung two men, all that were left of the crew. One, Hugh Owens, was alive when cut from the rigging, the other, Rice Parry, had died of exposure, being frozen to the rigging. His body was cut free and brought back. After retiring from the Lifeboat service, Robert served as Pier Master for thirty years, on Clacton Pier, and was eighty years old when he died on Sunday, September 20th, 1930.

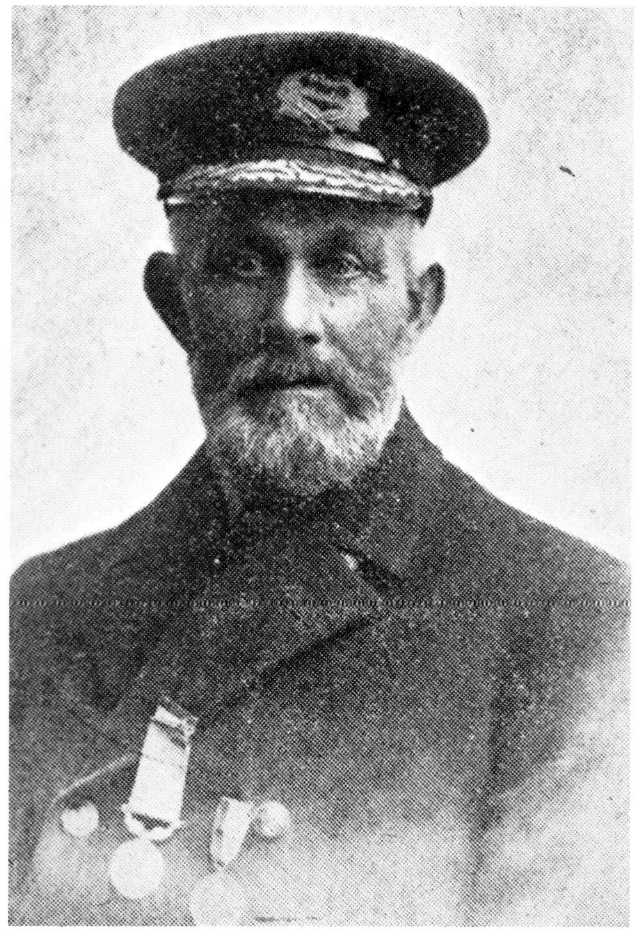

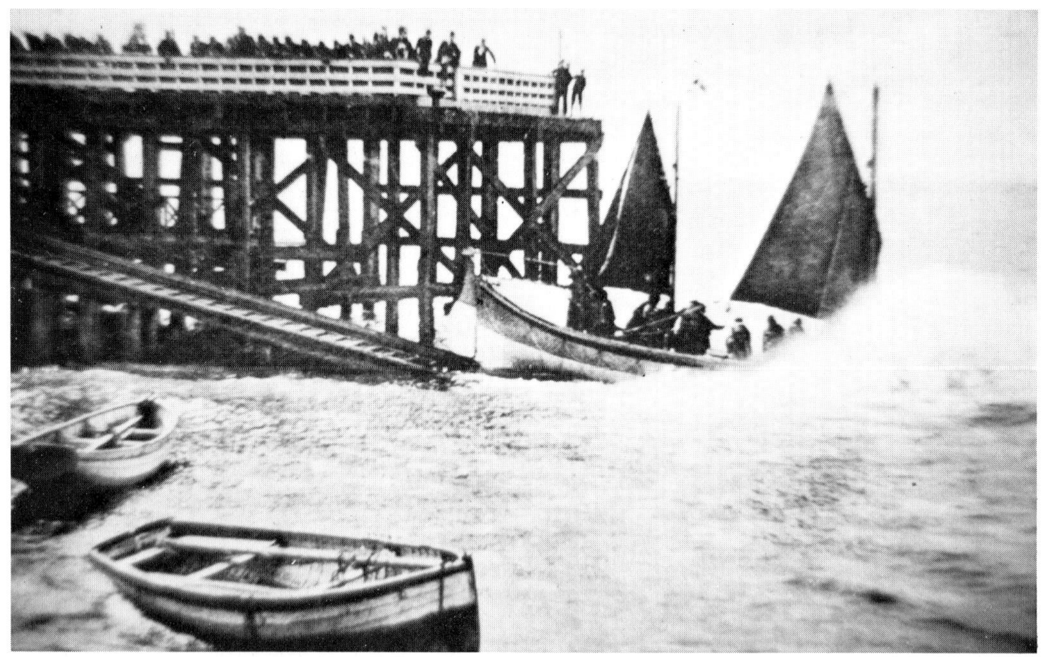

16. THE CLACTON LIFEBOATS – 1878 to 1914: 'Albert Edward' – (1878-1884), 'Albert Edward II' – (1885-1901) and 'Albert Edward III' – (1902-1929). The first of these lifeboats was 34′ in length, had ten oars (five each side) and two lug-sails. After her capsize in 1884, her Cox'n, Robert Legerton, advised that a larger boat be sent to the Clacton station and this was done. The second 'Albert Edward' was 39′ in length, had a beam of 9′ and had twelve oars (six each side). She was the first lifeboat to be fitted with a drop keel which gave a uniform increase of draught of 14 inches. She was a great improvement both in stability and sailing performance, and Robert Legerton spoke very highly of her. 'Albert Edward' – the third of that name – was sent to the Clacton station on 1st February, 1902. She was of the 'Watson' Class being 45′ long and 12′ in the beam, so being a lot larger than her two predecessors. Although a sailing craft in the first instance, she was later fitted with an auxiliary motor. The lifeboat being launched here with both sails set, is the second 'Albert Edward'. Note the rudder in the raised position. It will be lowered into position when clear of the slip-way, as would the drop keel. Her sailing rig shows a lug-sail on the fore-mast, with a gaff-rig on the Mizzen. Her crew reported that 'She sailed like a bird.'

17. SAVED BY A WHISKER! John Greer was a Commissioned Boatman in the Coastguard Service and became a member of the lifeboat crew when the first lifeboat came here in 1878. On 23rd October, 1881, he was with the crew when the 'Albert Edward' went to the aid of the French lugger 'Madeleine' aground on the Gunfleet Sands, and breaking up fast. A heavy sea caught the lifeboat and smashed her down across the lugger's deck, which enabled the lifeboatmen to haul aboard most of the crew. A ship's boy was pulled in by a boathook as he was being washed away. Another French sailor was being swept past; threw up a despairing hand, and found something to hang on to like grim death. What he had grasped was John Greer's beard as he leaned over the lifeboat's side. 'The sensation of having a man clinging to my beard was not all that pleasant... I reached over to scizc him, and instead he caught hold of my beard. He pulled my head down until it was under water. The man never let go until he was rescued. Yes! I had a bad face for some time afterwards, but it got alright again...' he told a reporter, stoically. John Greer was with Robert Legerton in the lifeboat when she capsized in 1884. 'That was about midnight and nearly nine miles from the land. The second Cox'n Cross, and Cattermole were drowned, but the rest of us managed to get back into the boat after she had righted herself.' The photo shows John Greer wearing his award from the French Government and his Silver and Long Service medals (RNLI).

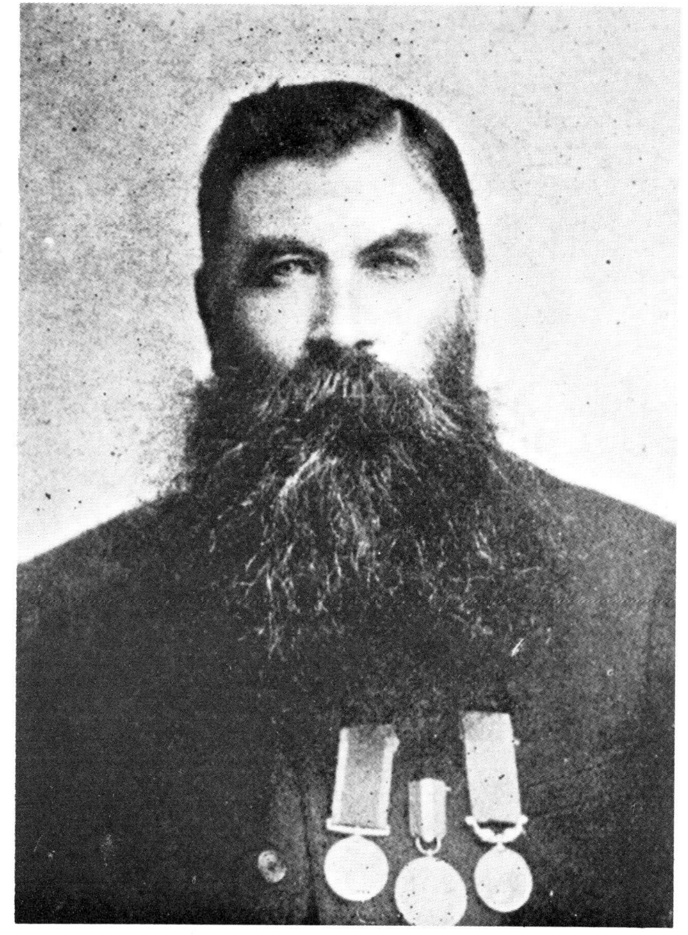

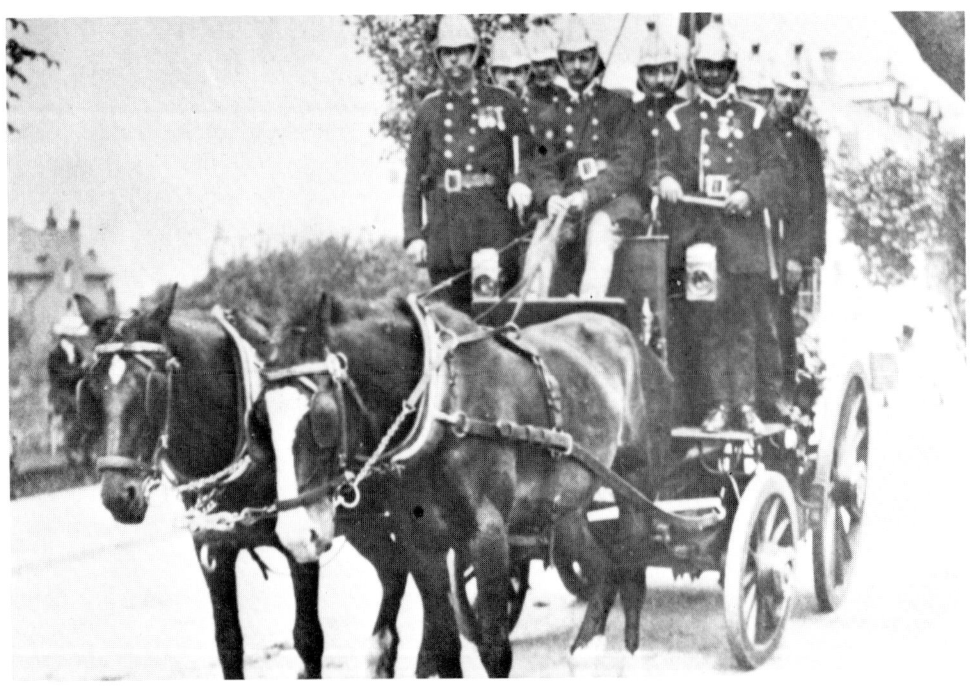

18. FIRE! FIRE! In 1892 the Clacton Local Board purchased a 'First Class Steam Fire Engine'. The steam presumably operating the water pump. In March, 1894, following several disastrous fires in te Board built and opened a Fire in Skelmersdale Road near the Railway Station. Six years later, the Council established a Town Yard, or Highways Department adjoining their Waterworks in Old Road, and here a new Station was provided, housing this the original horse-drawn Fire Engine, which served the town for twenty-seven years. The proficiency of this Volunteer Brigade was rewarded when, in June, 1905, they won the coveted Clinton Shield at the old Crystal Palace. The Chief of the Fire Brigade was Captain C.F. Hill. These are probably the famous horses who knew the difference between the Fire Brigade Bell and the Life-Boat Bell (see No. 11). As this is a special occasion, for they are all wearing their Medals, could it be in 1905, after they had just won that 'coveted Clinton Shield'? Their Superintendent was D. Wall, and the rest of the team at the Crystal Palace event were: F. Mathams, J. Puddy, A. Reed, H. Land and G. Jeffers, known to all as 'Darky' Jeffers, who later became the Chief.

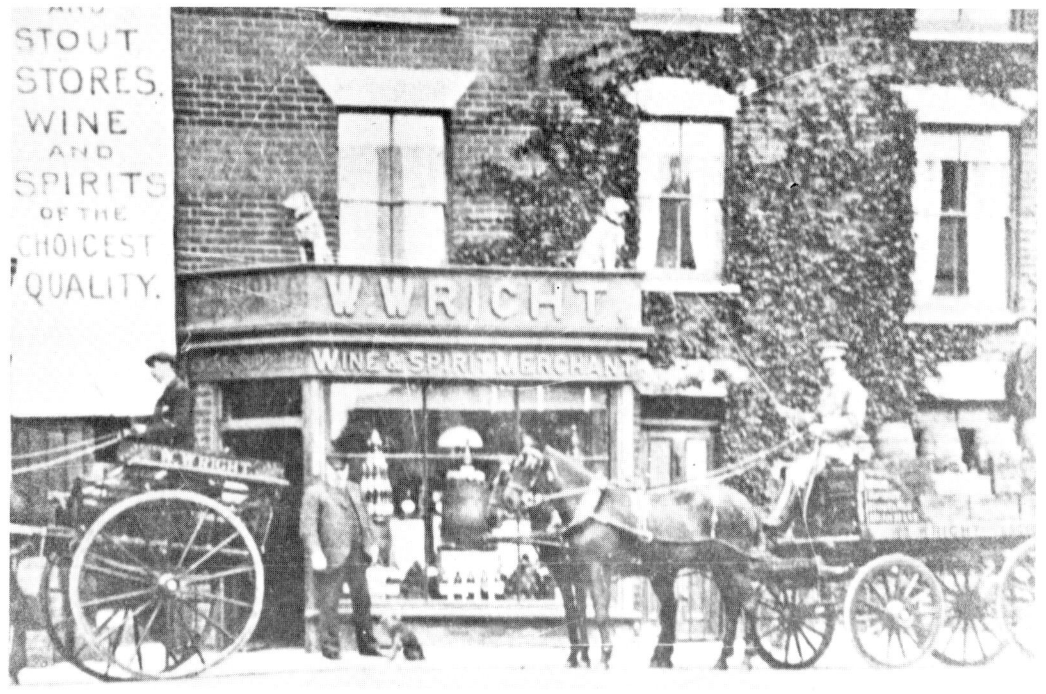

19. This is Rose Cottage, one of the oldest houses in the new 'watering place' of Clacton-on-Sea, for it was built in 1872, in Rosemary Lane, between the 'Osborne' and the 'Imperial'. In a 1901 Guide to Clacton it was claimed to be the oldest house. The two Osborne Hotel villas were being built in January 1872, so these were probably the first dwellings to be built in the 'new' Town. Rose Cottage was taken over by William Wright in 1886 to sell Wines and Spirits, and the shop still survives in Rosemary Road. This is a carefully posed picture showing two of Mr. Wright's delivery vans, the driver of the right hand one in uniform, with whip at the correct angle. Possibly the gentleman with the sitting dog is Mr. Wright himself. If you look carefully at the centre window on the first floor you will see a female figure; is it the lady of the house watching the proceedings from behind the curtains with great interest? Note also the two large ornamental dogs on top of the protruding shop front.

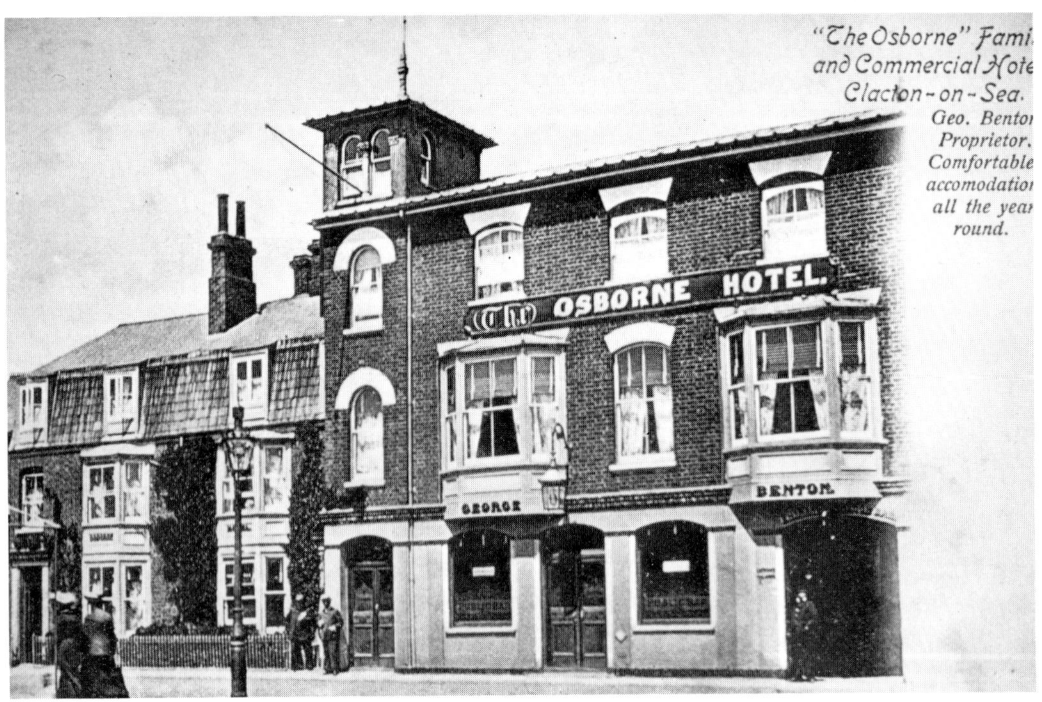

20. OLDEST VILLAS AND OSBORNE HOTEL. In 1871 Mrs. Frances Greenhill, the wife of a Colchester tailor, purchased part of the garden of a cottage and by the end of that year she was erecting a pair of villas on the site which were ready for occupation early in 1872 so, although the 1901 'Guide to Clacton' claims Rose Cottage (see No. 19) as the first house to be built in the new town, that distinction should more properly go to these two villas, seen here on the left. The 'Osborne' itself began life as a private residence known as Osborne House. It was taken over by William Middleton of Colchester in 1876 and became (The) Osborne Hotel. He added on the adjoining block with the turret in the following year in imitation of Queen Victoria's famous Osborne House on the Isle of Wight which has a similar turret. This postcard dates from mid-Edwardian times and George Benton's establishment was a very popular 'Family and Commercial' hotel in those days. When under different ownership, the then landlady's son, a daring youth, is said to have ridden his horse up the Hotel's steep stairs for a wager.

21. Above: EAGLE CRESCENT. This handsome crescent, built in 1880, curves round from Marine Parade East into Beach Road. The houses in it had just been occupied at the time of the 1881 Census, and this view cannot be long afterwards. The roads are unmade and there is only a primitive attempt at kerbing.

Below: ORWELL ROAD – EARLY TERRACE HOUSES AND DETACHED VILLAS. This photograph shows typical early development building in Clacton for these terrace houses (middle right) and the semi-detached houses on the left hand side of Orwell Road are quite new at the time it was taken in the late 1880's. Looking up Orwell Road, you can see the 'Osborne Hotel' in Rosemary Lane. The gas street-lamp is on the corner where the road joins Marine Parade East. The roads and footpaths are unmade although kerb-stones have been laid. The making up of the various roads in the centre of Clacton began in 1891. The building on the front right of the picture was a lecture hall before it became Harman's Estate Agent's Office.

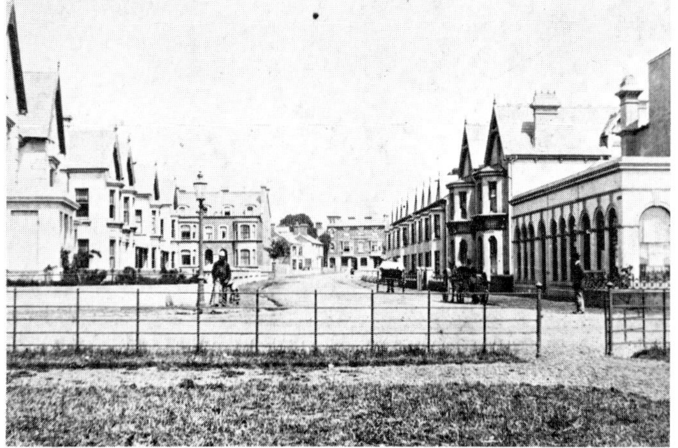

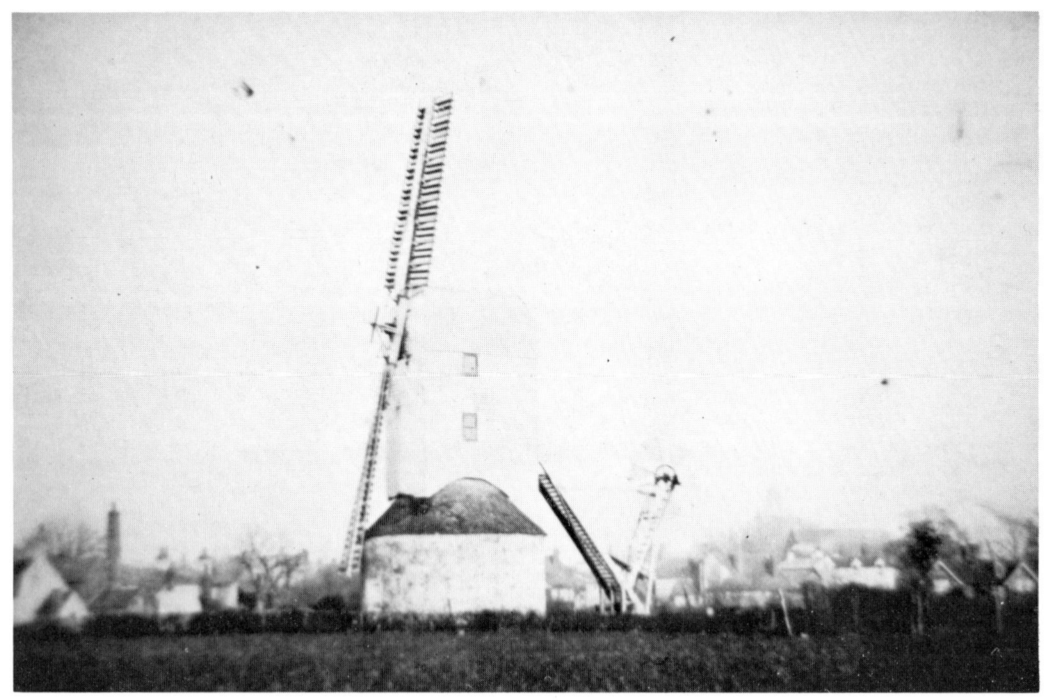

22. BROMLEY'S MILL (GREAT CLACTON). In 1867 Mr. Charles Beckwith erected a steam mill in Old Road (now Denco's) and at that time this old Post Mill was still working. It was a fine example of this type of mill where the whole of the upper part revolves on a central post so that the main sails are kept facing the wind. This is done by vanes at right angles to the sails which automatically shift the upper part of the mill when the wind veers. In 1886 Mr. H. Bromley took over the Steam-mill and the Post-mill from Mr. Beckwith. *Prior to Mr. Bromley taking possession, in May, 1888, the Mill had been closed for 2 years, and the old Windmill had ceased to work...* (Clacton Graphic, 1909). It still stood, gradually falling into disrepair, until it was demolished in March, 1918. Windmill Park and Mill Fields are reminders of its existence. *A predecessor was located up Thorpe Rd and was blown down one stormy night. The genial miller is said to have been playing there on his fiddle at the time, but emerged safely from an upturned window, fiddle in hand...* (K. Walker, History of Clacton).

23. Above: 'QUEEN'S HEAD'. GREAT CLACTON. Possibly named after Queen Elizabeth I, who twice stayed at St. Osyth's Priory, the home of John, Lord D'Arcy. On one of these she journeyed to Harwich and so could have travelled along this road, turning left up North Road. This postcard shows the smithy and the redoubtable Mr. Pigg, 'robust of frame and strong of limb', standing beside the rear horse. 'As well as carrying on a business as farrier, (he) became landlord of the 'Queen's Head'. During the time that Napoleon was banished to St. Helena, Mr. Pigg's grandmother 'became superintendent of his laundry, and was brought into touch with the fallen monarch.' To the right can be seen the horse-omnibus which operated between Great Clacton and St. Osyth until mid-Edwardian times. The fellow shoeing the horse is likely to be 'Bomber' Beaumont, who would shout very loudly 'Hold your leg UP.' The horses knew him and often lifted their legs up before he shouted. During the Napoleonic war there was a military presence at the school field in North Road and elsewhere and 'The fine, large room with bay windows at the 'Queen's Head' was built for a ballroom during the time the military were stationed here' (about 1809).
Below: THE MANSION HOUSE, GREAT CLACTON. On the opposite side of North Road to the 'Queen's Head' The Mansion House was probably built about 1720. It was demolished in 1966. For many years it was the home of the Field family, i.e. William Field, of Great Clacton, who married Arabella, illegitimate daughter of Richard Savage, 4th Earl Rivers, a noted general in Marlborough's time. Their son, William Field the younger, became the leading local attorney, and lived from 1709 to 1783. At the time this photograph was taken, not long before it was demolished, part of it was being used as an Antiques shop.

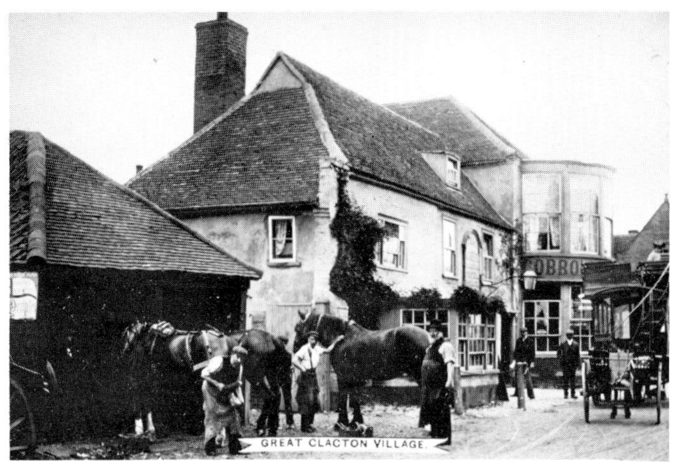

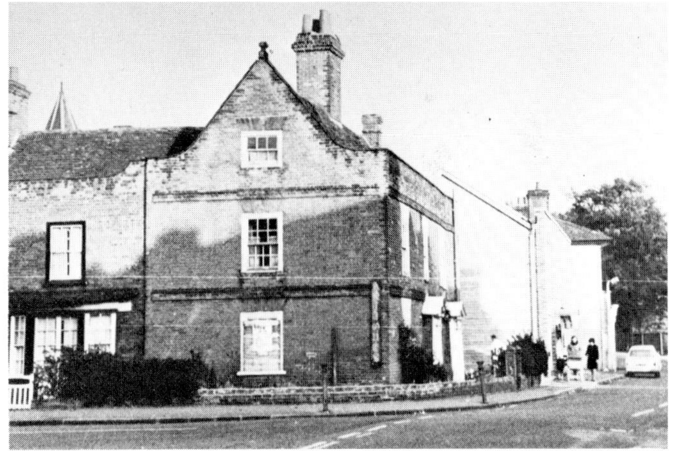

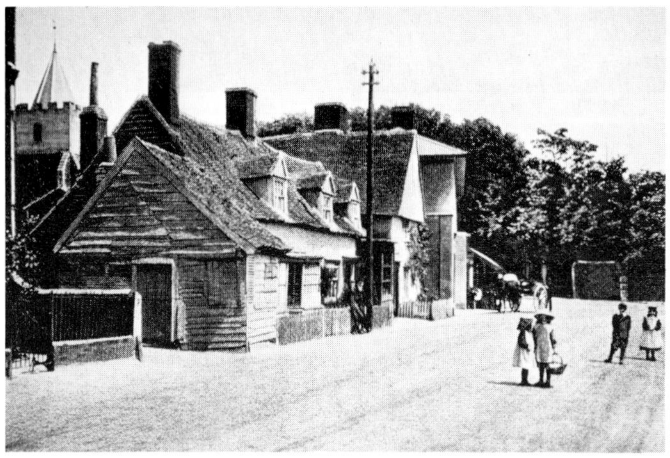

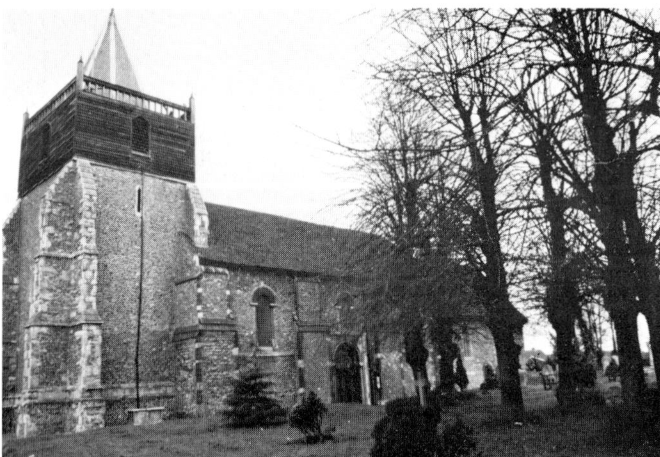

24. Above: THE VILLAGE, GREAT CLACTON. Great Clacton village abounded in such cottages as these in the eighteenth and nineteenth centuries. At the time this picture was taken in mid-Edwardian times, there were still several, but the last were pulled down in the 1960's. A peaceful scene in those days, where children need not worry about standing in the middle of the road, oblivious to traffic, because there was very little and you could always hear a horse and cart coming. To-day, just where they are standing, a pedestrian crossing has had to be installed to enable people to get across an extremely busy road. Note the crenellated top to the belfry of St. John's Church (left, background). This was damaged circa 1913 and replaced by the present top (see picture below).

Below: ST. JOHN'S CHURCH, GREAT CLACTON. Parts of this Church date back to the time of Richard de Belmeis who became Bishop of London in 1108. K. Walker writes that *Richard Beaumeis visited Chich, which at that time formed part of the domain of Clachenton where he had a house.* The tower dates from the fifteenth century (early) but it was never completed because the Abbey's finances were in a bad way. It is now capped by a weatherboard belfry. The previous picture shows the crenellated top which was damaged and replaced by this present structure about 1913. The remains of Roman bricks and tiles have been incorporated into the main fabric of the walls. One of the peal of five bells is inscribed 'Miles Gray made me, 1649', the year King Charles I was beheaded. Eleazar Knox, son of the famous Scottish reformer John Knox, was Vicar of St. John's from 1587 until his early death in 1591. The font is six hundred years old.

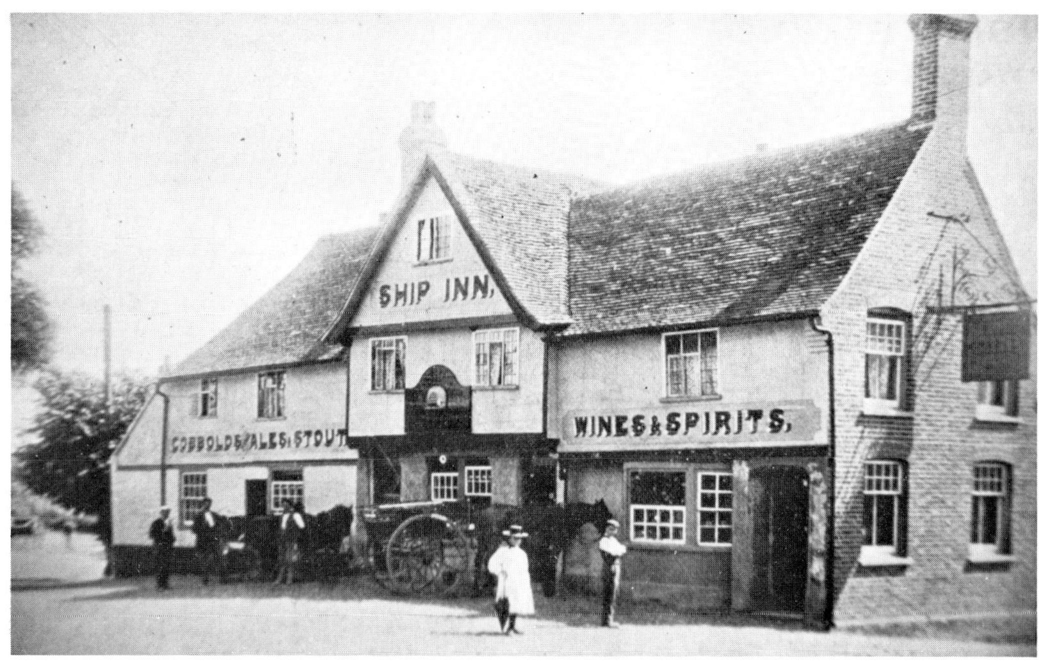

25. THE SHIP INN. The 'Ship Inn' was built about 1520. It is near 'Eaglehurst' in Valley Road, which was built in the nineteenth century by Dr. Thomas Harding Newman around the notorious smugglers haunt of a certain Captain Webb. Great Clacton was a centre of smuggling in the eighteenth century, and many a cargo of spirits, silk, tea or tobacco was landed on its desolate shores. Being so handy nearby, it is possible that the 'Ship Inn' was Captain Webb's 'local' and may have had a touch of the forbidden merchandise. Rumour has it that there are subterranean passages beneath the old village; from the Church towards St. John's Square; at the Hall; the Ship Inn, Eaglehurst and the Queen's Head. If they existed it cannot be ruled out that such convenient hidey holes might have been used by smugglers. One Summers day in 1797, a French privateer was forced onto the shore by a Revenue Cutter. Its crew of 24 Frenchmen were rounded up after a chase and to celebrate their success the victors gathered that evening in the 'Ship' where they consumed 400 pints of ale whilst the tale was told. In front of the 'Ship' and along the Street, a Fair was held each year on 29th June – St. Peter and St. Paul's day – it was abolished in 1872 after a life of over seven hundred years. (K. Walker – 'History of Clacton'.) But the 'Ship' and its nautical connections still survive.

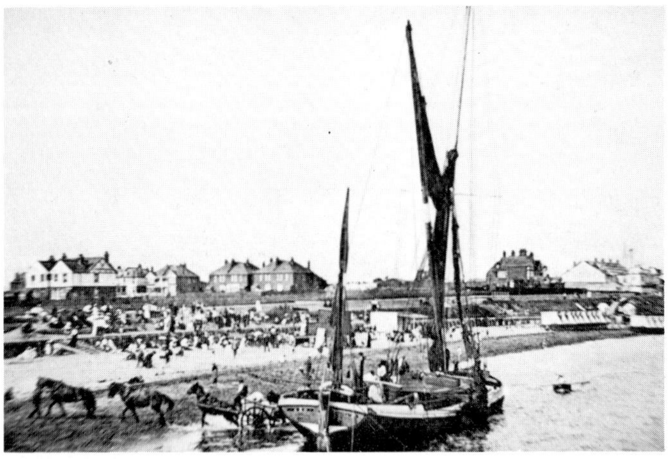

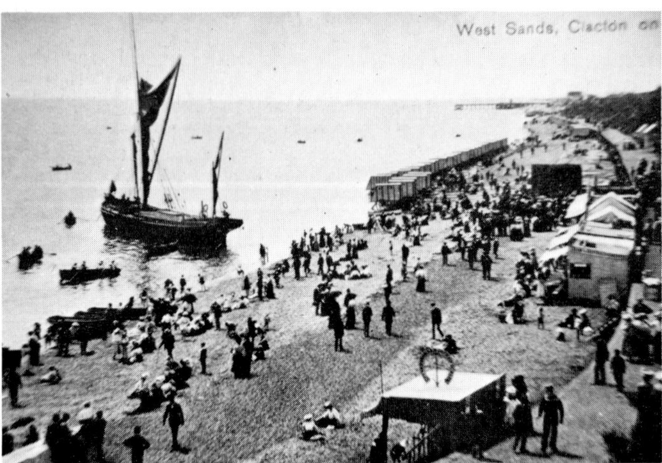

26. HOW THE THAMES BARGES UNLOADED AT CLACTON. These photographs show how the barges unloaded their cargoes, which were mostly building materials such as bricks, sand, cement, timber, etc., and flints for making up roads. The first photograph is of the barge 'Ash'. You can see that they need three horses to pull quite a small cart up over the sand and shingle onto the Wash Lane. Such a method of unloading was alright in mild conditions but was a hazardous business if the weather turned nasty. Waves could break right over the hull and the barge could be lifted up and thumped down on the shingle, rather as would happen if she were aground on the Gunfleet Sands, a fate which in those days 'shivered the timbers' of many an unfortunate ship. In such an emergency, those barges with a cargo of bricks used to resort to the desperate expedient of 'taking out the plug'. The barge filled up and was no longer bounced up and down on the beach. Alright with some cargoes but not with something like cement! The cargo had to be unloaded between one high tide and the next, when the barge would be ready to sail off in ballast. This moment is about due in the second picture. We can tell that the tide is coming in because the first half dozen in the line of bathing machines have been winched slightly up the beach, the rest of the line will follow. When the tide has risen sufficiently for her to float off, the Thames barge will hoist jib and tops'l, then unbrail and sheet home the loose footed mains'l and set the mizzen. The barge's spreet can be seen going up at an angle on the starboard side (right) of both main and mizzen masts. The jetty, built in 1898 to handle commercial cargo, can be seen at the top right of the picture. It was not much used by the Thames barges which preferred their usual method of unloading cargo onto the beaches.

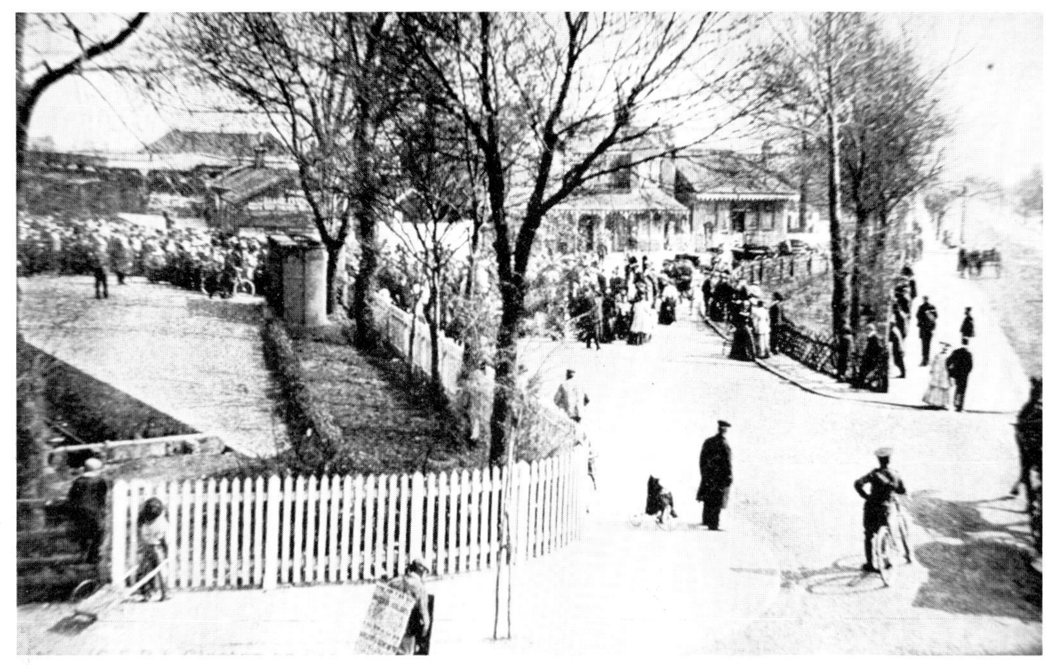

27. CLACTON'S FIRST RAILWAY STATION. After the Pier was built in 1871, it was the Paddle Steamers that provided the first direct run to the new resort, but it was not long before the railways took up the challenge. In 1877 the 'Clacton-on-Sea Railway' was incorporated to build a line from the town to link up with the G.E.R. and Tendring Hundred line which terminated at Thorpe-le-Soken. This connecting link, a single line until 1941, was opened on 4th July, 1882. *A great many absent,* wrote the Headmaster in the Gt. Clacton School Log Book on that day, *they went to see the first train to Clacton-on-Sea* – and doubtless suffered for it the next! Next year, 1883, both the Tendring Hundred line and the Clacton-on-Sea Railway were absorbed by the Great Eastern Railway. Competition between the Steamer Coys. and the Railway was fierce, with the former charging 4/6d return against G.E.R.'s 5/0d. Both offered excellent catering facilities. From 1910 the G.E.R. ran Pullman cars on some of its trains as well as Restaurant car expresses. There was also the famous 'Supper Car Express' which left Liverpool Street Station at 12.03 a.m. on Saturday nights and arrived in Clacton at 1.50 a.m. These first weatherboard buildings remained in use until the present Station came into use in 1929. The old G.E.R. became part of the L.N.E.R. in 1923.

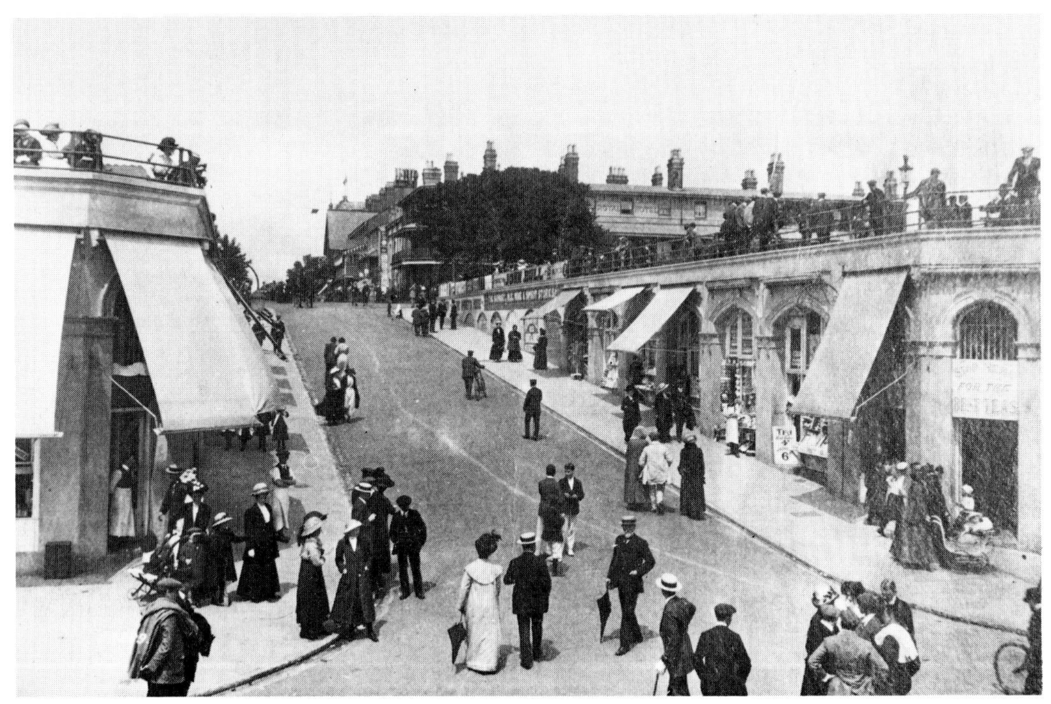

28. 'CURTAIN UP'. This photograph has something of the quality of a play just about to begin. A sort of 'Curtain-Up' feeling. It was taken looking up Pier Gap in 1912 and is historic in that it was possibly the last to be taken showing this sort of scene with the shops open for business on either side of the Gap. The 'Clacton Graphic' on 23rd November, 1912 reported that *The Clacton Council, having purchased from the Coast Development Corp. the shops on either side of the road, which was converted into a Public Highway some two years ago, contemplate the sweeping away of the business premises and generally beautifying the sea entrance to the Town.* Eventually, they were all replaced by a landscaped rock wall, rocks and shrubs, whilst a bridge, first known as the 'Rialto Bridge' but later changed to the 'Venetian Bridge', was built about half way up to link the East and West Promenades. The 'Boater', which came into vogue as Gentlemen's headgear a few years earlier, is very much in evidence.

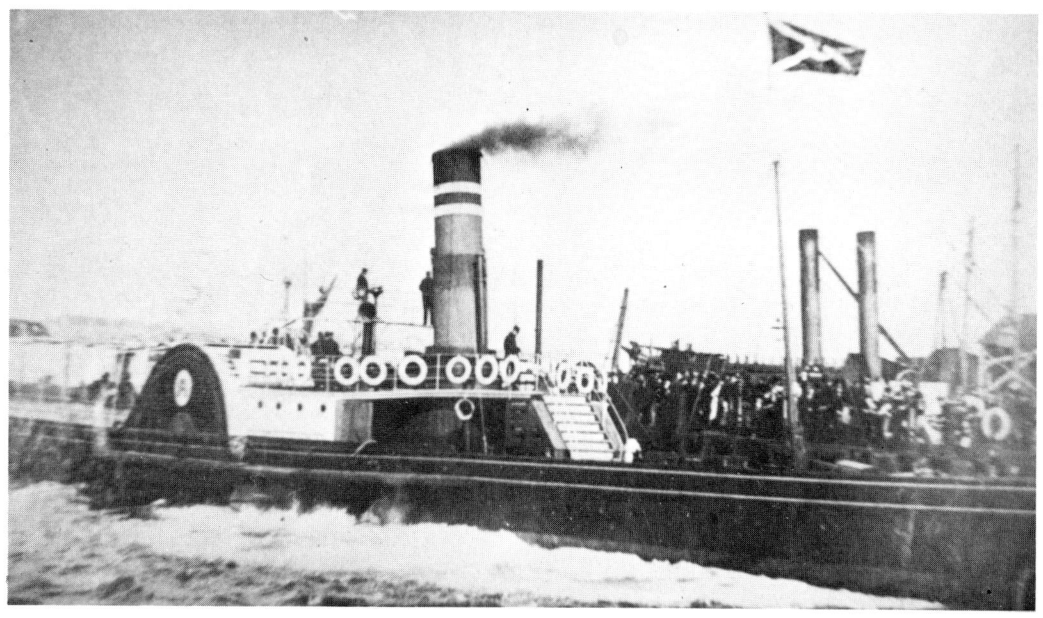

29. THE PADDLE STEAMERS THAT HELPED BUILD CLACTON. The Paddle Steamer 'Glen Rosa', built in 1877, began her life in Scottish waters. In 1881 she was sold to the Thames and Channel Steamship Coy., and then successively acquired by the London Steamboat Coy., and the Victoria Steamboat Association Ltd. and was put on the Clacton run in 1884 by the V.S.A. In 1888 she was the first excursion steamer to do the double journey from London to Clacton and back in the same day. Unlike most excursion steamers the 'Glen Rosa' was not tied to any one route but was run on various services. At one time, for example, she ran from Yarmouth to Harwich so as to connect with the 'Koh-i-Nor' on the Harwich-Clacton-London run. She also ran from London to Southend and Sheerness, but in 1896 she was sold to a Bristol Coy. and went out of the East Coast services. Another of these early Paddlers was the 'General Havelock' *having,* as Kenneth Walker writes in his 'History of Clacton', *a barrel of drinking water on deck with a tin mug tied to it with string, while a fiddler used to entertain the passengers.* However, the 'Glen Rosa' was better and, in a handbill dated July, 1881, was advertised as 'having a speed of 22 miles per hour...' and customers were invited to visit Clacton, Walton, Harwich or Ipswich, 'by the new and magnificently fitted steamer 'Glen Rosa' sailing from London Bridge, (Old Swan Pier), Thames & Channel Steamship Co.' Here she wears the funnel colours of the V.S.A., i.e. three narrow bands of white-black-white between the red of the funnel and its black top.

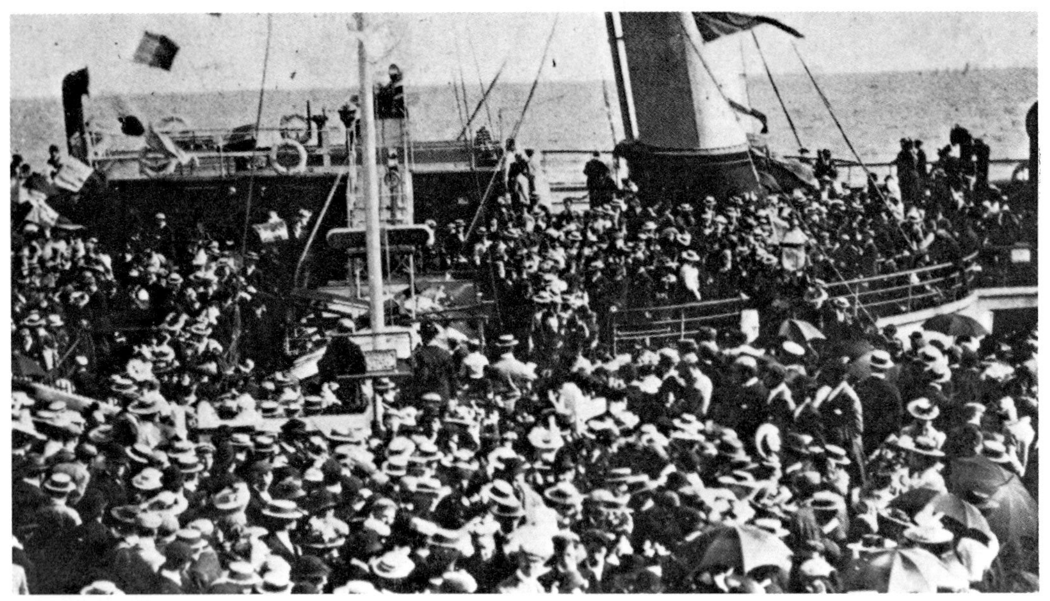

30. THE 'BELLE STEAMERS'. The saga of the 'Belle Steamers' began when the London, Woolwich and Clacton-on-Sea Steamship Coy. was formed in 1887. Their first Paddle Steamer, named 'Clacton', went into service on May 17th, 1888. After only one season she was sold and the Coy. turned to the firm of Denny Bros. of Dumbarton, who over the next ten years built them a fleet of seven light draught Paddle Steamers starting off in 1890 with 'Clacton Belle' which served on this run for close on forty years. Next year, 'Woolwich Belle' was launched to be followed two years later by the largest, fastest and most popular ship of the fleet, the famous 'London Belle'. 'Southend Belle' (later re-named 'Laguna Belle), followed (1895), then 'Walton Belle' (1897), 'Yarmouth Belle' (1898) and finally 'Southwold Belle' was launched at the turn of the century to complete the fleet of seven fine 'Belles'. All were built to a similar design with steel hulls topped by an upper, or promenade, deck which extended as far forward as the single mast. A navigating bridge was placed immediately behind the one buff coloured funnel. Mr. A. Fletcher was in the catering Department of 'Belle Steamers' and told me 'Practically all my trips were on the 'London Belle'... On one occasion, presumably at low water, we were delayed quite a while through getting stuck on the Gunfleet Sands and had to wait for sufficient water to get going again. The catering on board in those days was excellent; a table d'hôte four-course dinner could be had for half-a-crown.' Note the prevalence of the 'boater' on both male and female in this picture postcard.

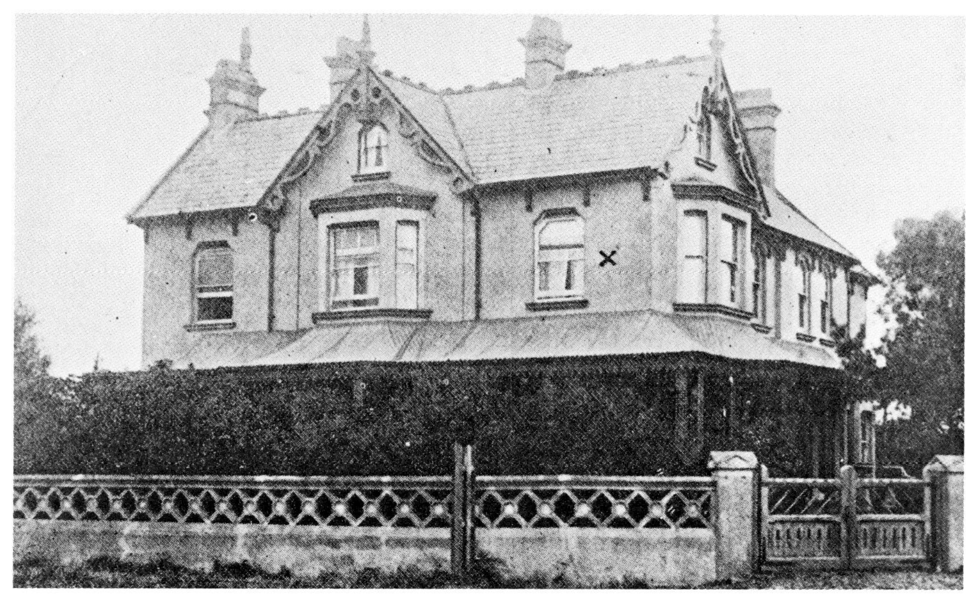

31. CROSSLEY HOUSE. James Harman, one of the town's pioneer figures, built a house called 'Ocean View' when he came to Clacton in 1874. It stood right at the eastern end of Marine Parade. About 1884 he conveyed it to General William Booth, of the Salvation Army who, with his wife Catherine, made it into a home of rest for their officers. Catherine Booth had a great love of the sea and in 1888, when it was found that she was suffering from cancer, she stayed for some time at 'Ocean View'. Through the generosity of Frank Crossley, one of the Salvation Army's great benefactors, General Booth was able to rent the house for his own use in 1889 and brought his wife down to live in it and spend her last few months by the sea. She was able to take short walks along the cliffs or drives in a carriage. The cross by the window marks the room in which she was confined to her bed in October of that year. It had a view out across what was then known as the 'German Ocean' (North Sea). Her little grand-daughter recalled 'There seems to be many strangers in the big house, I feel safest in the garden to which I can go by the side door near the housekeeper's room.' Catherine endured her suffering with great fortitude until the morning of Saturday, 4th October, 1890. There had been two days of thunder, lightning and torrential rain, but the weather had cleared when she passed away peacefully, at the age of 61. The Salvation Army established themselves in Clacton in 1897. Sir Savile Crossley (afterwards Lord Somerleyton) presented the house to the Eastern Counties Institution as a nursing home in 1895 and in recognition it became known as 'Crossley House'.

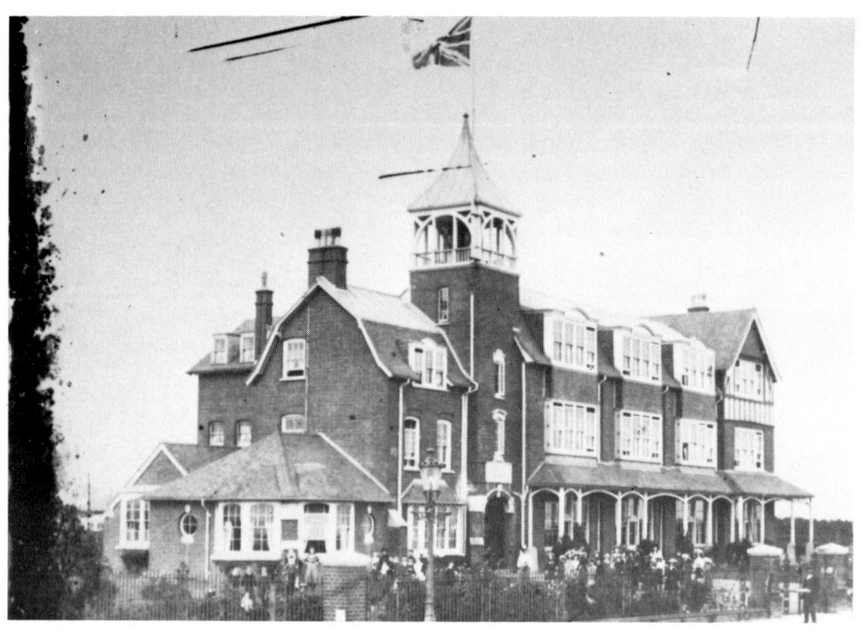

32. THE PASSMORE EDWARDS CONVALESCENT HOME. John Passmore Edwards was born in the tiny Cornish village of Blackwater, in 1823. He grew up to become the proprietor of many popular newspapers and journals, and lived by his own creed: 'He is a wise man, who in his lifetime, so spends his wealth that by it men and women bless his name before his death.' He became the Member of Parliament for Salisbury in 1888 and was a keen political reformer. When the Sunday School Union began their scheme for holiday homes for deprived children, John Passmore Edwards became an enthusiastic supporter, contributing £6,000 for a home to be built for this purpose at Clacton-on-Sea. On May 19th, 1898, Sir H.H. Fowler M.P., laid the foundation stone with these words: 'The Sunday School Union is proud to avail themselves of the opportunity and unite in their grateful acknowledgement of his munificent offer – to make possible a permanent holiday home for the benefit of Sunday scholars needing a change of air and scene.' The Passmore Edwards' Holiday Home was officially opened on June 23rd, 1899, and the great philanthropist himself died in his 88th year in 1911. This photograph, taken about five years after the home had been opened, is from a damaged glass negative used, for many years as a garden cloche, but rescued some fifteen years ago. Signs of wear and tear can be seen on the left, and in the scratch marks.

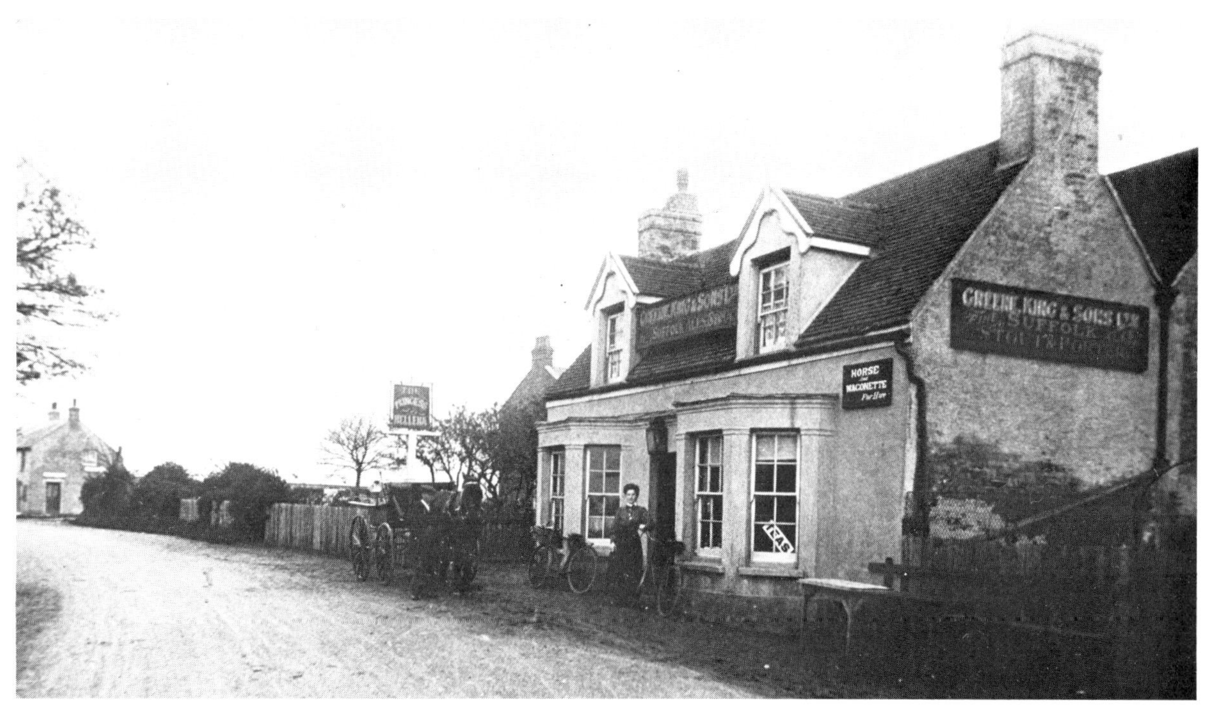

33. THE 'PRINCESS HELLENA', LITTLE HOLLAND. Licensed as 'The Beerhouse' in 1882. Plans for the future development of Little Holland, a small village some two miles to the east of Clacton-on-Sea, went ahead at the turn of the century. A map of the 'Preston Estate' in 1904 shows the proposed roads which included Kings Avenue, Kaisers Grove, and Kings Cliff. Probably when Greene, King & Sons took over the little beer house, shown in the photograph, in 1883 from its previous owner, one Fleetwood Codd, they decided to maintain the regal note. There were two Princess Helenas. Princess Helena Victoria (1870-1948), a grand-daughter of Queen Victoria's, and Princess Helena (1846-1923) who was her mother and the fifth child of Queen Victoria. At the time this photo was taken, in 1905, Little Holland was all farmland except for a few agricultural cottages. In 1934 it was absorbed by Clacton and became Holland-on-Sea. A year later the 'Princess Helena' was pulled down and a large new Public House called 'The Roaring Donkey' replaced it. (Note spelling: 'Hellena' on sign-board.)

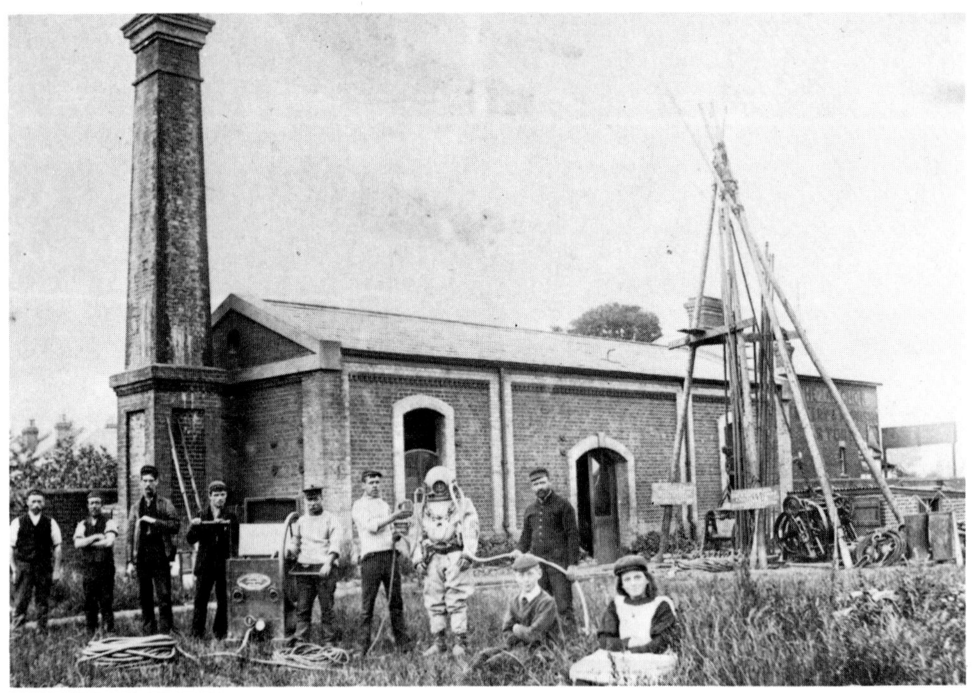

34. DON'T FORGET THE DIVER. This is an intriguing photograph, taken in 1895 in the Town Yard off Old Road. The building at the extreme right is not connected with the central building and chimney and has 'The Anchor Grocery & Provision Stores', written on its walls. There is a well beneath the sheerlegs erected to the right. The two notices inform us that this is the 'Clacton-on-Sea Gas & Water Comps., A. Penfold, Esq. Chairman., J.C. Webb, Engineer' (right hand notice). The other notice carries a name like 'I. Taley & Sons, Water Works Engineers'. The Council acquired both the Gas and Water undertakings together with the works in Old Road in 1899. Abel Penfold, who died in February 1900, was chairman of the Pier Co., Gas & Water Co., Royal Hotel Co., Steamboat Co., Public Hall Co., and the Clacton Land Co. Penfold Road is named after him. He died in the same year as Peter Schuyler Bruff. The diver is just about to have the round glass face piece put on which is held by the man on his left. Next are two men either side of the air pump. This would be Clacton Water works pumping station and the team, carefully posed and documented, is all set to send the diver down to inspect the well.

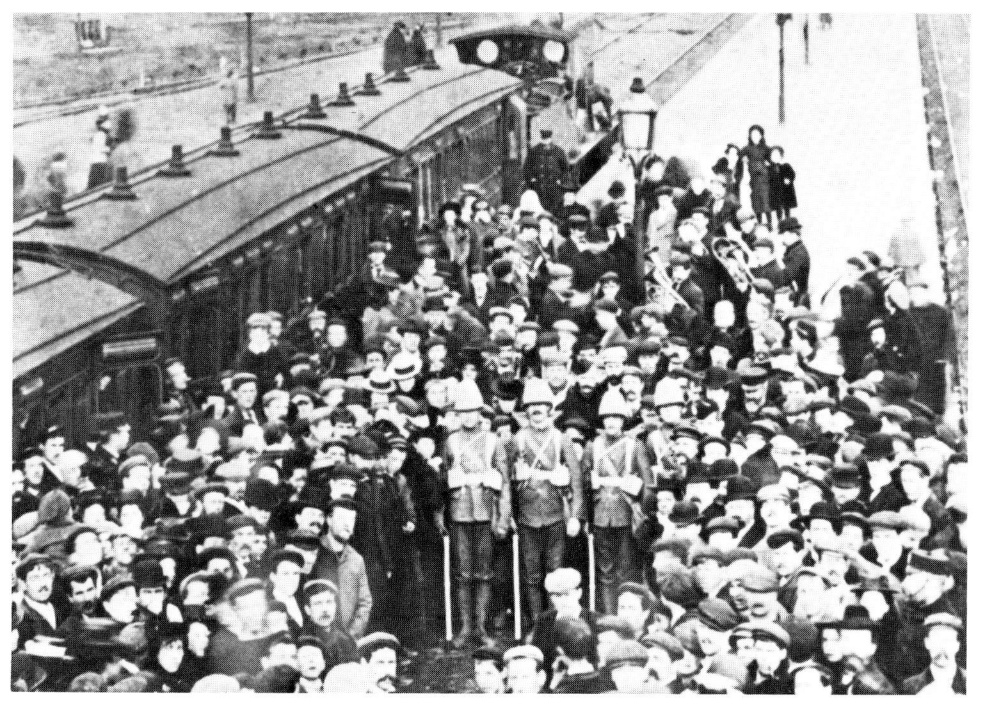

35. The scene at Clacton Railway Station on 3rd March, 1900, as 'The residents of the Town gave the volunteers a grand send-off to the war'. The war they are off to is the Boer War (1899-1901). They are from Company 'H' of the 2nd Volunteer Battalion, The Essex Regiment, based in Clacton.

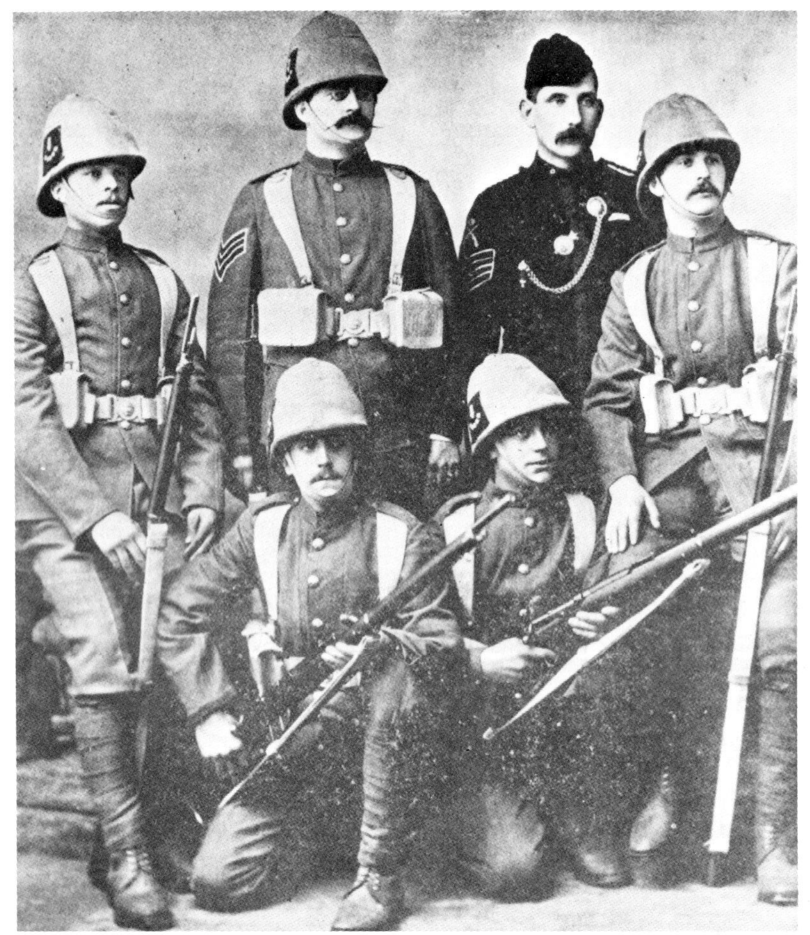

36. Clacton volunteers for the front. Kneeling, left: Pte. G. Skeels, right: Pte. W. Harman. Standing, left to right: Pte. W. Flegg, Sgt. A. Quick, Sgt. Instr. Hodgson and Pte. E. Bates. Sgt. Abraham Quick, with waxed moustaches, produced the 'Clacton News' which first appeared in 1889. In later years he became Councillor Captain A. Quick, M.B.E., and was Chairman of C.U.D.C. in 1926. Pte. W. Harman returned to Clacton in October 1900 after a severe attack of enteric fever.

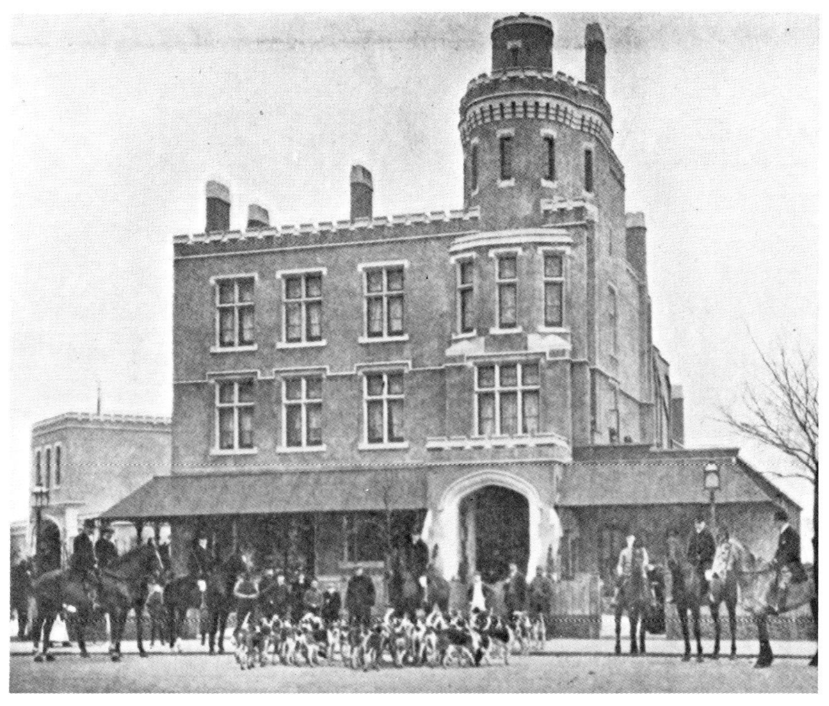

37. THE WARWICK CASTLE HOTEL. Designed and built in 1896 by W.J. Hook, as a form of grandiose hotel. Unfortunately it was built in the wrong place, right at the end of Pier Avenue where it joins Old Road and some distance from Marine Parade. (The site for all the major hotels of the town because of its proximity to the sea front, and the view of the sea to be had from seaward facing hotel rooms.) It had an impressive, but imitation, castle-likeness. The North-East Essex Fox Hounds used to meet there on occasion as in this photograph of late 1899. In later years it was the venue for Car Club rallies and Concours d'Elegance. The Warwick Castle Hotel was demolished in 1974 to make way for a large office block, which never got built!

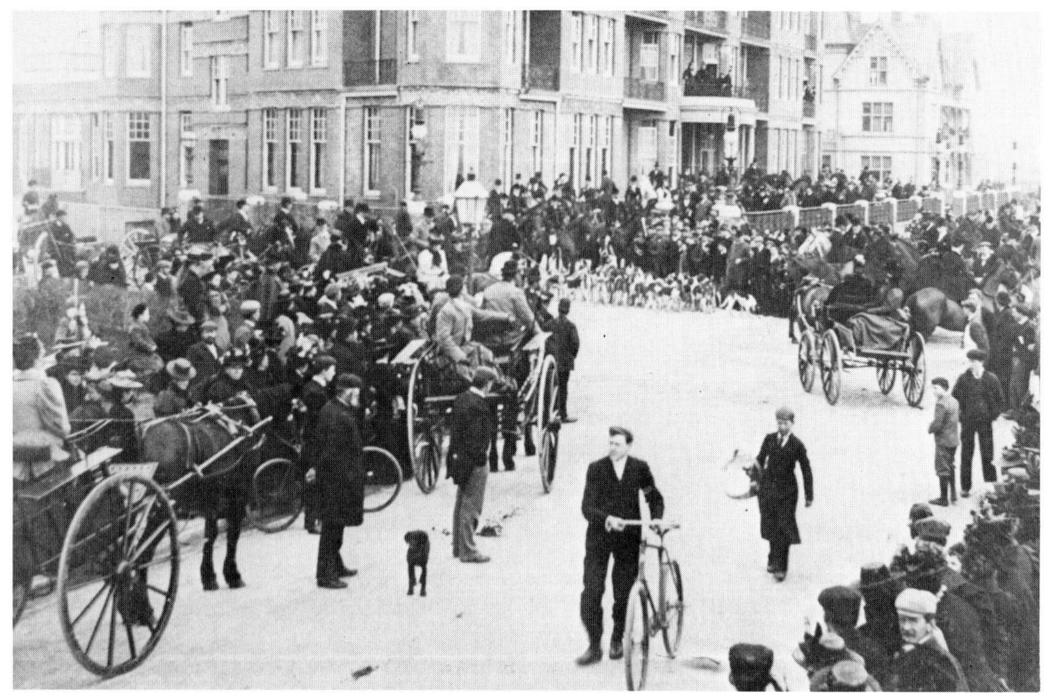

38. Another venue for a meet of the North-East Essex Foxhounds was at the Grand Hotel, Marine Parade, Clacton, on Boxing Day. This one is on Boxing Day, 1901, after a 'white Christmas' with a fall of 2-3 inches of snow. The stirrup cup has been passed around and the hunt is just about to move off into the open country along to the right of this photograph at Little Holland and Holland marshes. Among the male spectators the general head-gear seems to be baggy caps with narrow peaks. One chap seems all set to mount and follow on his bike. A quite smartly dressed errand-boy marches briskly behind him. A Labrador Retriever puppy (centre left) shows his breeding by turning his back on the whole proceedings. Pony Carts and Traps abound. Not a 'Horseless Carriage' in sight. The Grand Hotel itself had been opened in 1897 at the time of Queen Victoria's Diamond Jubilee. The Towers Hotel, just beyond on the right of the picture, was opened six years earlier, in 1891.

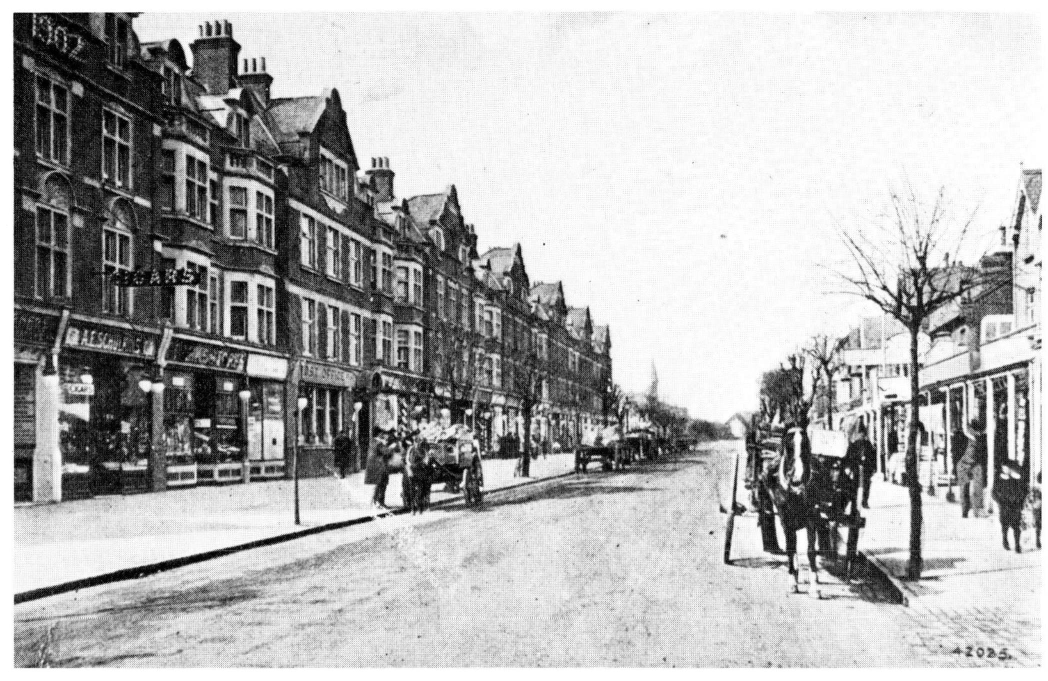

39. ELECTRIC PARADE. This line of shops and premises was built in 1901 and opened, as can be seen by the date picked out in electric lights at the top of the first building on the left, in 1902. It was known as Electric Parade because it was lit throughout by the new 'Electric Lighting'. In the centre, just behind the first horse and cart on the left, can be seen the new Post Office (now W.H. Smith's), which was moved there from the old premises in Station Road. Although the shops themselves have been greatly changed, the upper storeys preserve much of this Dutch inspired gabled architecture. Mr. E. Newson's 'Gentlemen's Outfitters' shop was No. 17, Electric Parade, and the firm still occupies the same premises. Clacton Council at the time was undecided about adopting the new method of lighting. 'It is a notorious fact that they are removing the electric light from the streets of many towns and putting in gas again...' said one Councillor. Another was 'Convinced that electric lighting would never pay...' But in the end they voted to submit a scheme for a local government enquiry. This picture was taken in the winter not long after Electric Parade had been built.

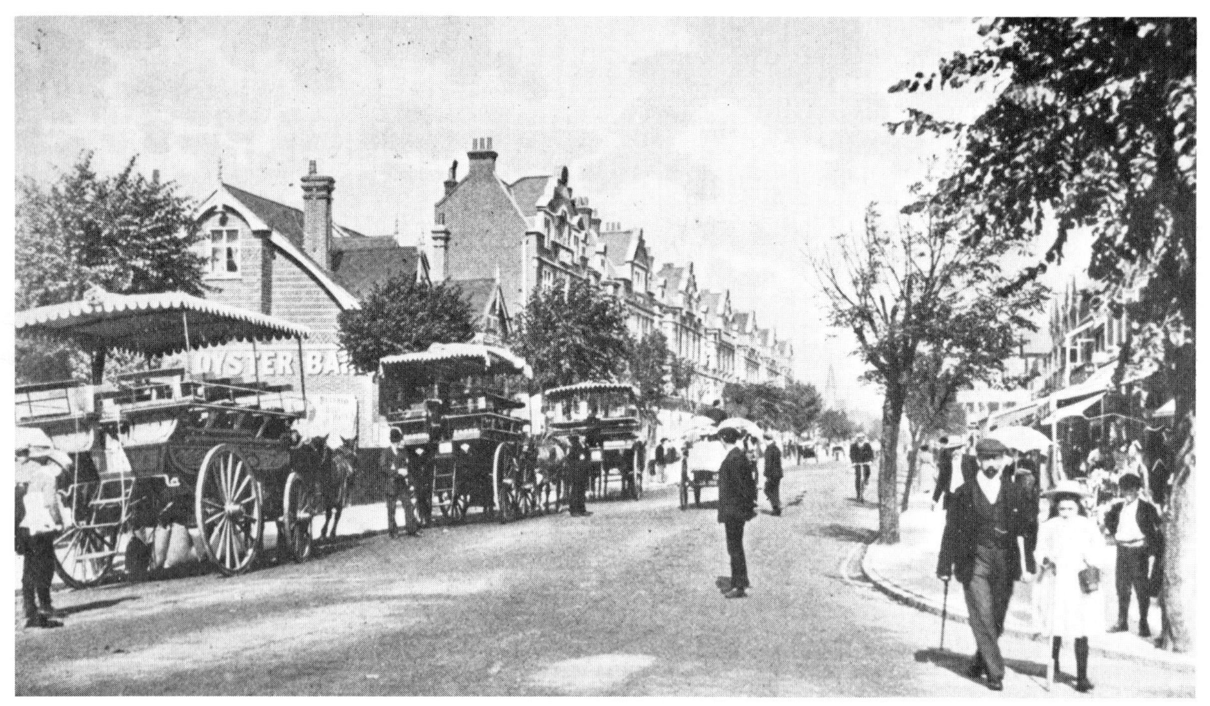

40. ELECTRIC PARADE (2). The trees are a bit bigger so it is probably about 1906. The three horse-drawn brakes (large waggonettes) yield a fascinating glimpse of how the 'Outings' of yesteryear were transported. The occupants of these may very well be in the 'Oyster Bar'. Just below the word 'Bar' is a poster advertising the famous 'Buffalo Bill' but where he was appearing is illegible. The gentleman on the right is taking his daughter down to the beach; she is well equipped with bucket and spade, also a skipping rope. The lad just behind, with arms akimbo, regards her with contempt; he appears to be smoking a pipe. It looks as though the lad on the extreme left is a newspaper boy, who has just trodden in a pile of horse-dung. Or is he looking down taking care to avoid it?

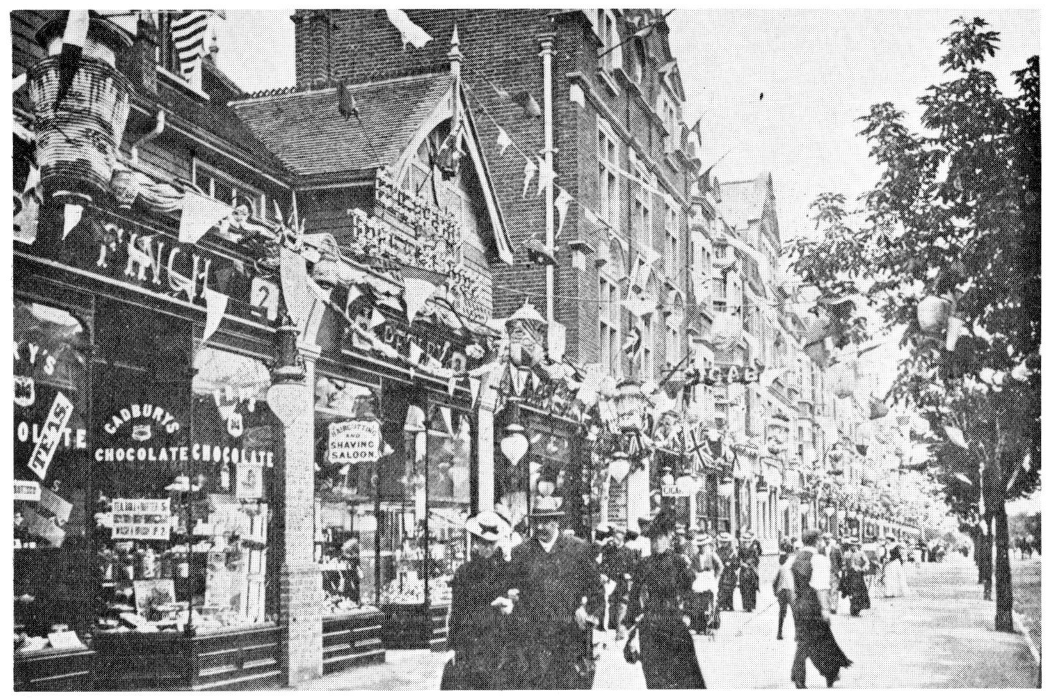

41. ELECTRIC PARADE (3). HIGH SUMMER. Photograph No. 39 showed a winter scene taken not long after Electric Parade was opened, indeed, the photographer does not seem to have been clear about the name for that postcard is captioned 'Electric Avenue'. The photograph above was taken in high summer, with a multitude of flags, bunting, Chinese lanterns etc. Could it be to celebrate the coronation of King George V which took place on 22nd June, 1911? The pear-shaped electric lights outside each shop can be seen very clearly. The trees, in full leaf, have grown quite considerably. A corner block, known as Central buildings, was erected in 1907 to the left of the two detached shops – Finch (Confectioners) and G.H. Petley (Shaving Saloon & Hairdressers). This is a very lively and animated scene.

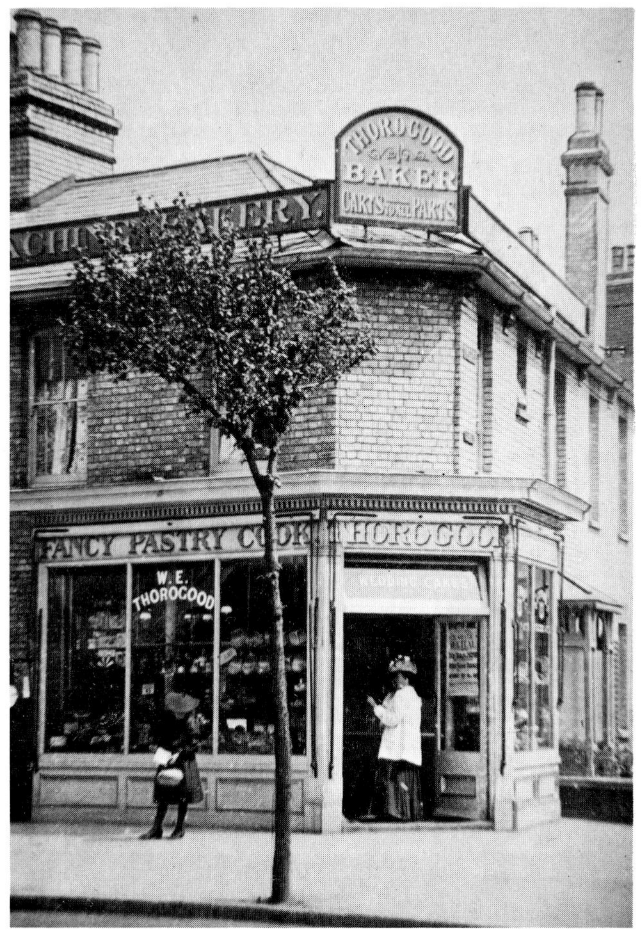

42. THE CORNER SHOP. A typical 'corner shop' of Victorian and Edwardian times. This is W.E. Thorogood's Baker's shop at the corner of Pallister Road and Station Road. On the notice board at the top of the building he advertises 'THOROGOOD – BAKER – Carts to all Parts'. In those days most shops operated their own delivery service to your front door. To be seen in the shop window along with the cakes and pastries, are Cottage Loaves, & 'Bloomers'. Currant Loaves were 6d and 'Wedding Cakes' are advertised on the door blind. On the door is a notice proclaiming a 'Dramatic Recital'. Those taking part include a Mrs. Barrow, Miss Lysa Brooks and the date seems to be Wednesday, May 10th, 19– although the last name and part of the date are hidden by the angle of the open door. The lady posing in the doorway wears a hat with a decoration of artificial fruits and flowers. The young girl by the front window wears a large Tam O'Shanter hat and is just checking her purchases. The shop is still there, but now it is a tobacconists and confectioners. It was the Town's first Post Office until moved to Electric Parade.

43. THE INVASION OF 'LETSPRETENDIA', 1904. In the early years of this century Britain began to take seriously the military threat posed by Germany under Kaiser Wilhelm II. An 'Invasion' exercise in 1898 was followed by the great Autumn manoeuvres of 1904, when a force of six cruisers covered the landing of two divisions which struck inland as far as Witham before being held and pushed back by the defending troops. They then retired to their landing places at Clacton and Holland-on-Sea and re-embarked. These manoeuvres are a fascinating microcosm of an age. The already famous were there, like General Baden-Powell and Field Marshal Lord Methuen, whilst General Sir John French (later Field Marshal, and G.O.C. of the B.E.F. in 1914) commanded the 'Blue' Invading army. Others, like Colonel Allenby, who 'conducted a brilliant little cavalry action', rose to high command and achieved fame as the captor of Jerusalem (1917). The photograph shows General Sir John French talking to the Admiral who commanded the Cruiser Squadron, Rear-Admiral Sir Wilmot Fawkes, at the foot of the cliffs near Pier Gap.

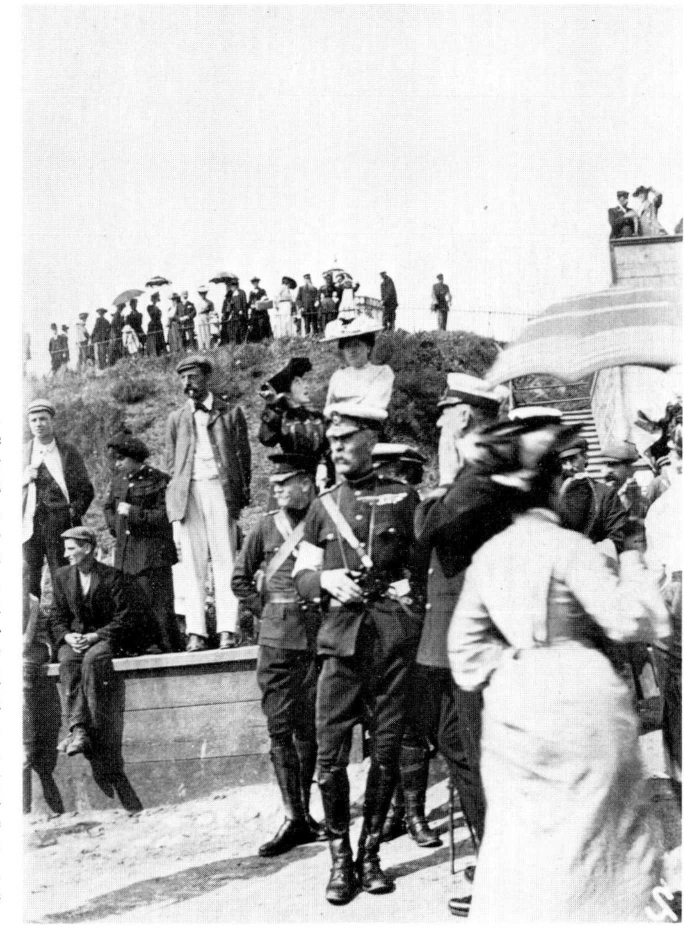

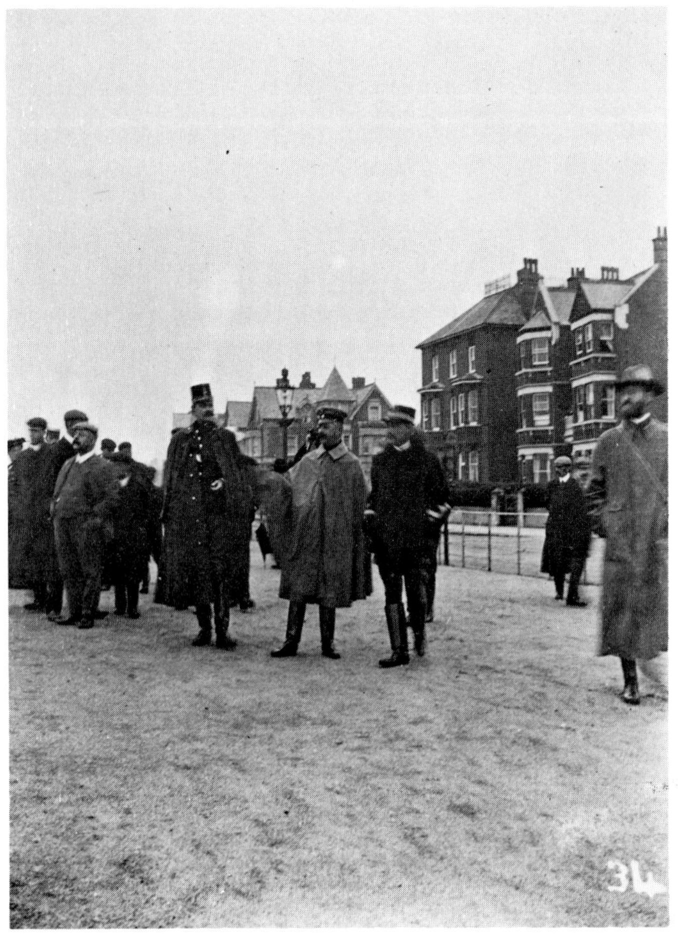

44. THE INVASION OF 'LETSPRETENDIA', 1904 (II). A variety of foreign military attachés 'in their variegated uniforms who are the guests of the king...' were transported daily from their accommodation at 'The George' Colchester, in a fleet of privately owned cars specially lent for the occasion. Here present on Clacton Cliffs are four of them. On the left is Major General Yermoloff of Russia who, 'in his huge car, with the French military attaché, was a hazard to all and sundry as he appeared and disappeared in a cloud of dust.' Next to him is Major Count von der Schulenberg of Germany, he later became Chief of the General Staff of the Kaiser's Garde-du-Corps, and was present at the fateful meeting when the Kaiser was advised to abdicate. On the right of this little group of three is the French representative, Colonel d'Amade. Ten years later, in 1914, he was the general who commanded 'Three French Territorial divisions... between the British and the sea', and performed an invaluable service by barring the way around the British left flank, in the long retreat from Mons. The United States attaché, Major J.H. Beacom, is standing on the extreme right of this historic photograph.

45. THE INVASION OF 'LETSPRETENDIA', 1904 (III). This photograph was taken at Holland Gap, where part of the 'Invading' forces landed. Up on top of the low cliff is the Duchess of Connaught, with her son, Prince Arthur. Field Marshal The Duke of Connaught, Inspector General of the Forces and Umpire in Chief at these manoeuvres, is first on the left of the group of three walking up the gap. He was the third son of Queen Victoria and was born at Buckingham Palace in 1850 (died 1942). He was made a Field Marshal in 1902 and served as Inspector General of the Forces from 1904-07. In the middle of the group is Rear-Admiral Sir Wilmot Fawkes, who commanded the six cruisers taking part. Of these 'Good Hope' and 'Monmouth' were to be sunk with all hands ten years later in 1914 at the battle of Coronel. Another, H.M.S. Kent, was with the force which pursued Admiral Graf Spee and, determined to avenge her sister ship 'Monmouth' burnt all her ward-room furniture to get the last extra knot to catch up and sink the 'Nurnberg'. On the right is General Sir T. Maxwell. At the time, Edgar Wallace was making a name for himself as a journalist and wrote some critical articles about the manoeuvres in the 'Daily Mail'. It was he who referred to Clacton as 'The Capital of Letspretendia'. He published his first best-seller, 'The Four Just Men', two years later in 1906. In the early 1890's, as a young man, he had worked as a labourer building houses in Wellesley Road, Clacton.

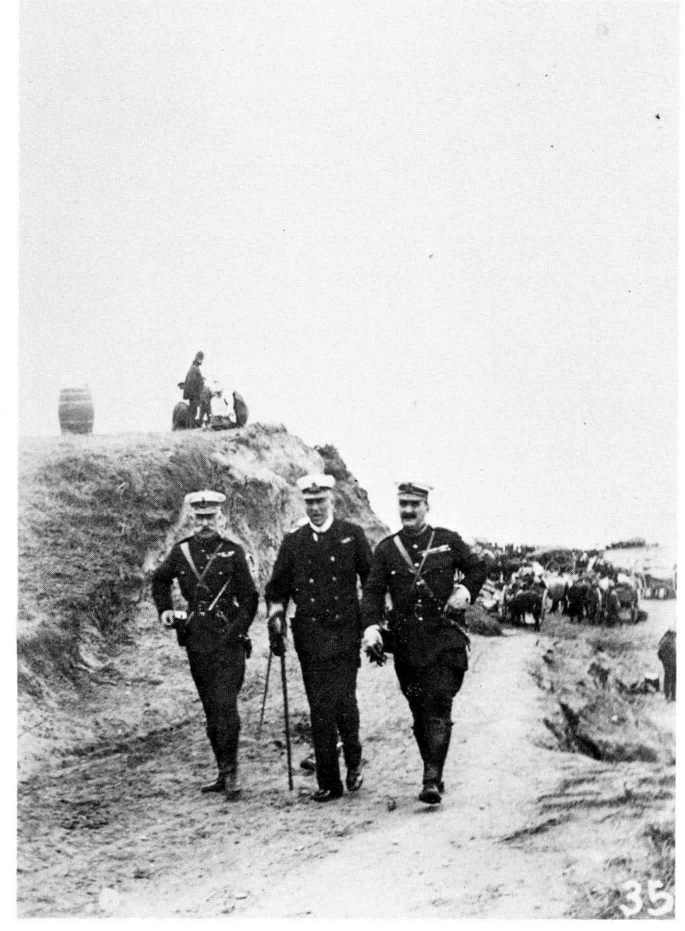

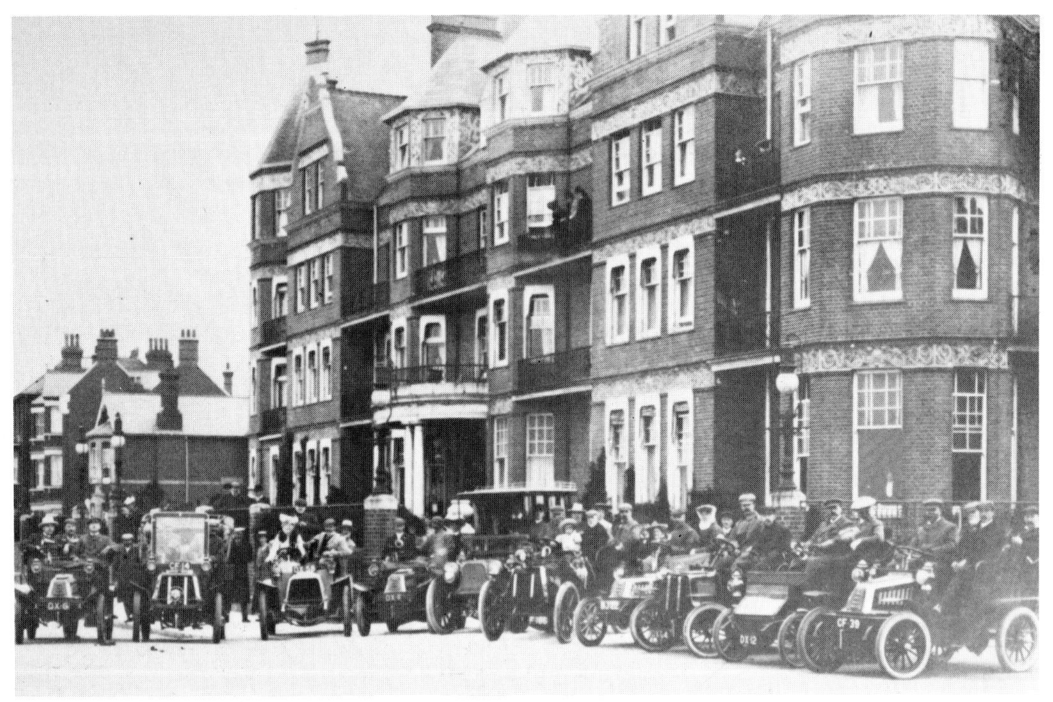

46. THE INVASION OF 'LETSPRETENDIA', 1904 (IV). Parade of the automobiles used to transport the Foreign Military attachés from their quarters in Colchester to Clacton and other places during the manoeuvres. They belonged to various wealthy people of London, Essex and Suffolk who volunteered their use for the occasion and enjoyed themselves with this impromptu 'Concours d'Elegance' after the manoeuvres ended on Thursday, September 15th, 1904. This is a unique photograph of vintage cars among which are two DE DION's (Reg. Nos. DX 6 and DX 11), a DARRACQ (Reg. No. DX 58), and a VOITURETTE (Reg. No. DX 12). All the cars were registered in 1904, and the registration of DX 6 was cancelled in 1905. The Grand Hotel can be seen in the background.

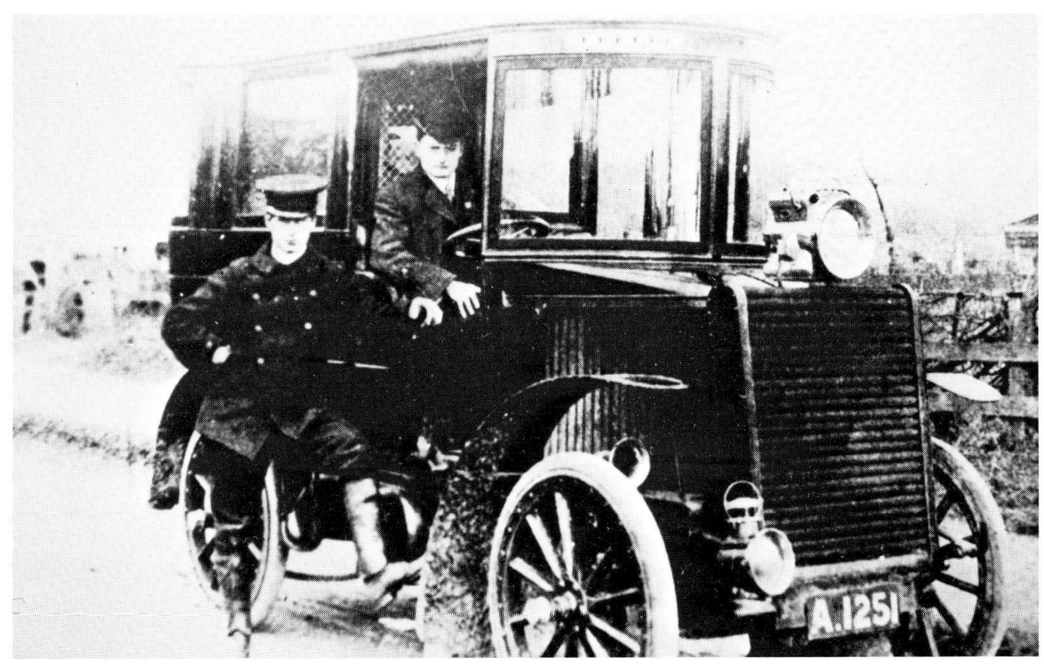

47. THE CLARKSON STEAM CAR. This extraordinary vehicle is the Clarkson Steam Car (with a Greater London Reg. No.). It was owned by a local businessman, who is seated at the wheel, and his chauffeur was Mr. G.M. Ephgrave, of Clacton-on-Sea. Thomas Clarkson was a Yorkshireman who took over the Moulsham Iron Works at Chelmsford in 1902 and turned out a number of steam cars and buses. He developed this 16 h.p. 'Steam Brougham' known as the 'Chelmsford' which could seat eight passengers. It had a multi-tubed boiler under the enormous bonnet, which was heated by paraffin burners. The resultant steam pressure operated a 2-cylinder double-acting engine. The size of the vehicle was against it becoming widely used for private purposes and its future development was in the field of public transport. The 'Clacton Graphic' (6th October 1906) carried an article on dress for chauffeurs: 'What is the correct way to dress one's chauffeur? A great number are in favour of dressing him like an ordinary coachman with a cockaded top hat; others prefer the motor cap and coat and leather gaiters. Speaking for ourselves we should be more agitated that he knew how to drive the car..!' The latter mode, of motor cap and coat and leather gaiters is obviously favoured here.

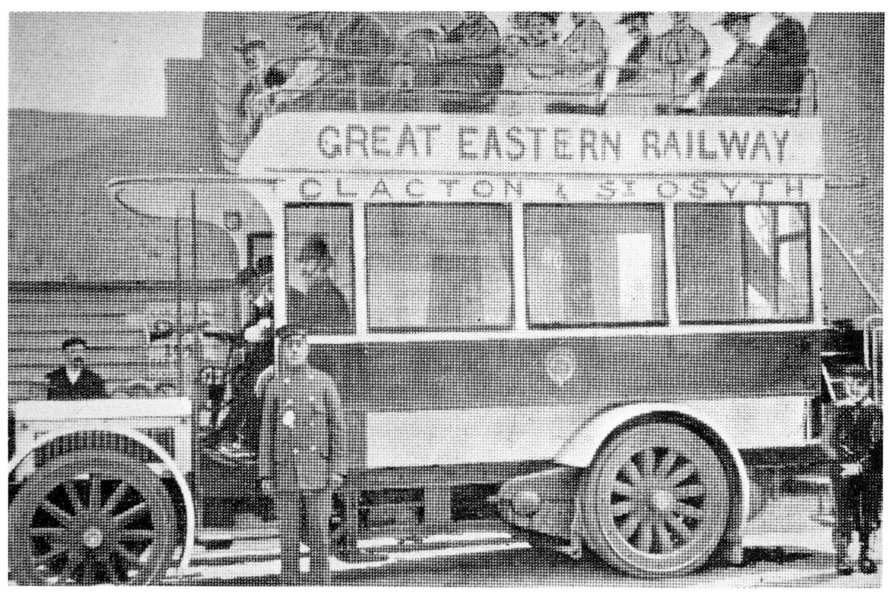

48. THE FIRST MOTOR OMNIBUSES. In 1898 The London Motor Van and Wagon Co. began negotiations with C.U.D.C. about running a 'Motor Cab' service in the town. Soon afterwards the first motorised public transport was running to the inevitable chorus of complaints about excessive speed and frightening the horses. The company replied that 'their drivers had already received instruction to drive their cars at a moderate speed through the town... the maximum speed which could be attained by the cars was 12 m.p.h...' In August, 1905, the G.E.R. began a 'Motor Bus service running between Clacton and St. Osyth. The engine is 4-cylinder and 30 h.p. The differential gears are of novel design, and the chains run in an oil bath, which is a novelty... The engine is fitted with a Simmsbosch low-tension magneto... The tyres are of the Sirdar buffer type, and are all solid... The body of the car is painted white enamel, and the interior is upholstered in blue morocco leather, and curtains to match. The fittings are mahogany, and there are sliding doors to exclude the dust. The windows, however, can be taken out and stored in a box at the back when desirable...' This looks to be the inaugural journey reported by the 'Clacton Graphic' on August 19th, 1905. All the passengers have crowded on top, to enjoy the novelty of this new mode of transport. The proud driver stands in front of his vehicle; two passengers pose behind the almost upright steering wheel, and there is a Policeman there to see that everyone keeps the peace. By the way: 'The car will carry 36 persons, and it is fitted with a locker capable of holding about one ton of goods.'

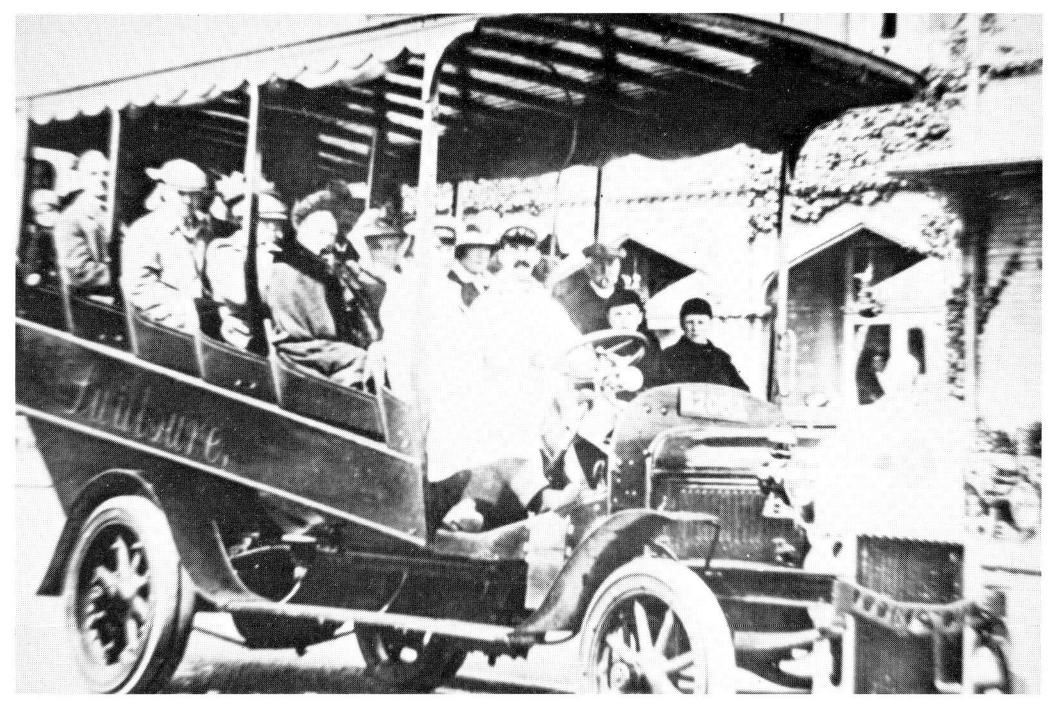

49. THE 'SWIFTSURE'. The 'Swiftsure', as can be seen, was of an unusual shape, a typical 'char-a-banc'. (French = benched carriage; an open coach with transverse seating.) It made its first run on Tuesday afternoon, 14th August, 1906 to St. Osyth. The return journey to Clacton was via Weeley Heath, Great Clacton, along Valley Road, back to the Middlesex Convalescent Home then along Marine Parade. The first Public Service run began the next morning. Built by the Lancashire Steam Motor Co., its 4-cylinder motor with low tension magneto ignition developed 35-40 h.p. However, this vehicle was not noted for its reliability and was known locally as the 'Neversure'. This picture shows Mr. C.F. Barnes at the wheel. He had the first (Public) Drivers Licence issued in the Town, and Barnes Coaches was the oldest Motor Coach Co. in Clacton. The London Motor Van and Wagon Co. began to run the first motor cab service in the town at Whitsun in the year 1898.

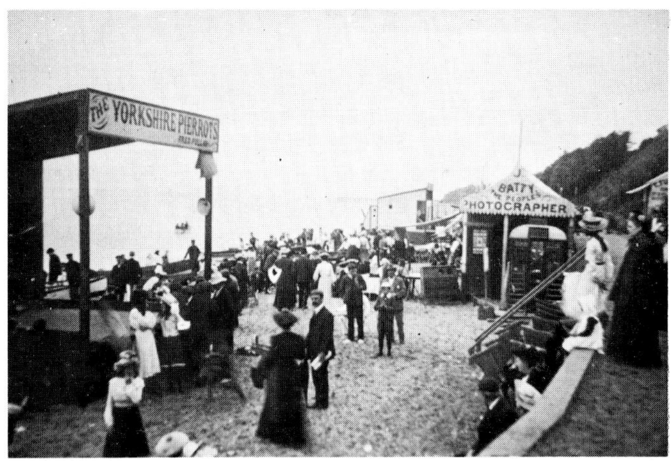

THE YORKSHIRE PIERROTS, West Beach, Clacton-on-Sea.

Proprietor - FRED PULLAN. 5th Season 1905.

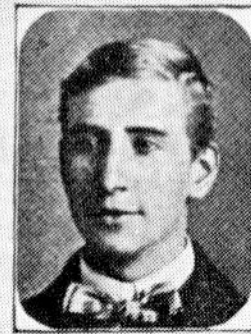
Phil Rabey.

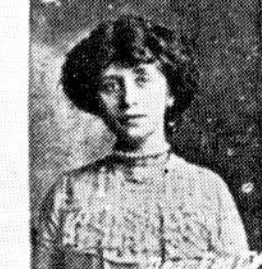
Mrs Fred Pullan.

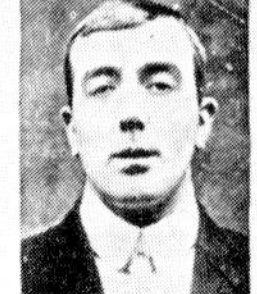
Alec Tyson (Pianist)

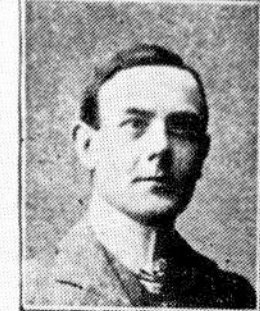
Louis Ackroyd.

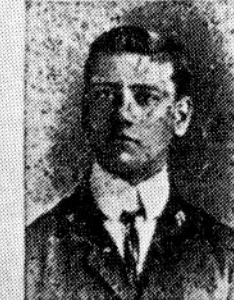
Harry Frewin.

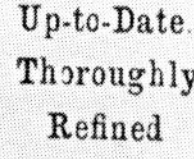

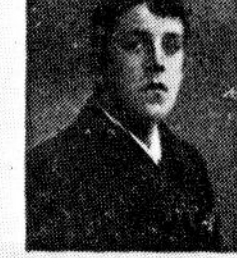
Frank Mackay

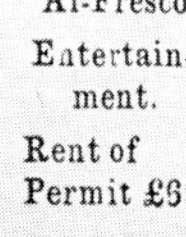

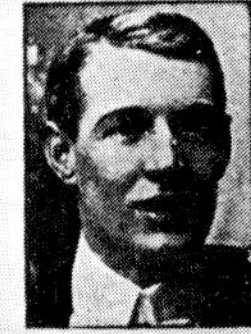

50. THE YORKSHIRE PIERROTS. This beach scene shows the alfresco type of entertainment provided for holiday makers. On the first stage, the Yorkshire Pierrots gave performances every week-day at 11 a.m. and 3 p.m. Another stage near the Jetty housed 'Harry Frewin's Jolly Coons'. Generally speaking, the Yorkshire Pierrots held pride of place in the visitors affections, possibly because it was nearer the Pier. Fred. Pullan was the proprietor and his wife was one of the performers, the others are named on the second photograph. The Yorkshire Pierrots opened in Clacton in 1901 and as will be seen Harry Frewin was still with them at the time of their fifth season in 1905. He left in 1907 to start his own 'Jolly Coons' Co. Alas for the Yorkshire Pierrots, on Tuesday, 6th August, 1912, in a gale, the 'rough seas lifted the stage right off the piles', and that was the end of Mr. Fred. Pullan's beach show.

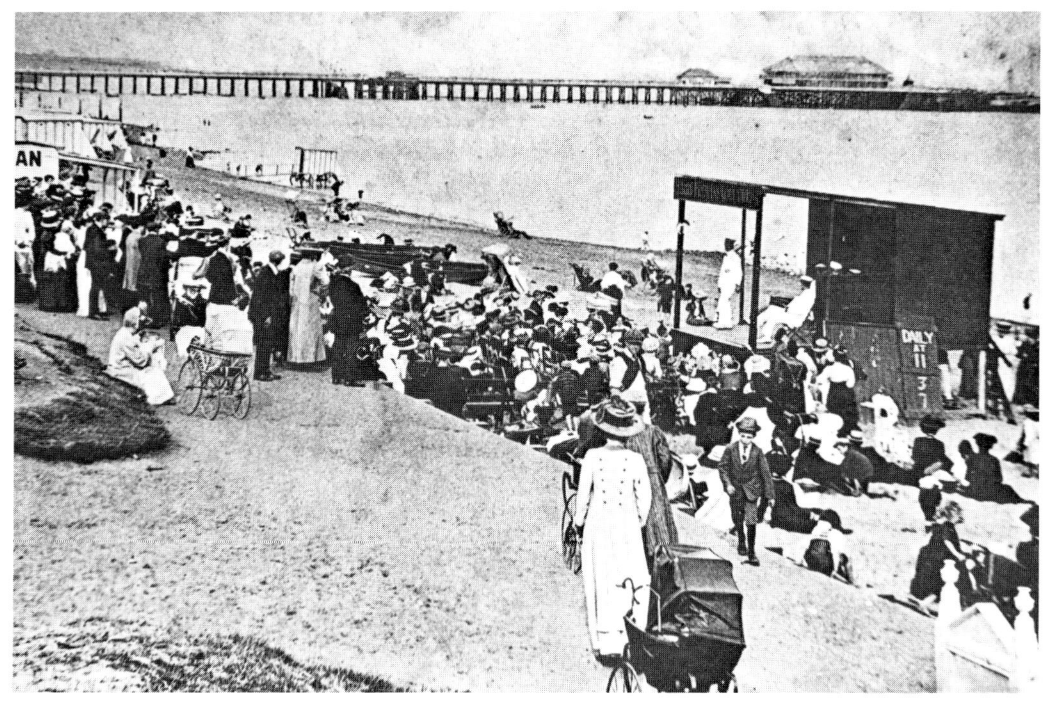

51. THE 'JOLLY COONS'. At the other end of the West Beach down near the Jetty, Harry Frewin's 'Jolly Coons' put on three performances daily at 11 a.m., 3 p.m. and 7 p.m. The 'Clacton Graphic' in its issue dated 18th July, 1914, reports *The Jolly Coons are going great guns at the Jetty Promenade and are well supported by visitors to the town. The company includes Messrs Tich McCoy and Dan Lyons (light comedians) Fred. Wallis (illusionist) Max Prinzen (musical speciality artiste and roller skate expert) Percy Mackey, and, of course, the ever popular proprietor Harry Frewin.* It looks as though the light comedians Tich McCoy and Dan Lyons are on, doing their act, in this picture. It was described as 'a smart, refined show'.

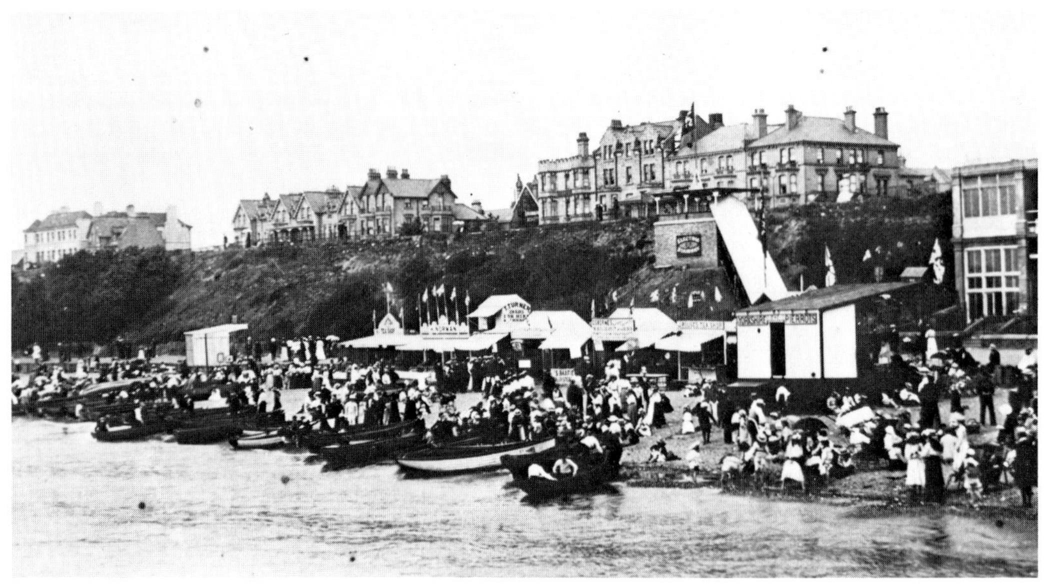

52. BEACH SCENE AND 'RENO' ELECTRIC STAIRWAY. A crowded beach scene in mid-Edwardian times with, from right to left, the Yorkshire Pierrots stage; J. Rouses Tea Shop; Osbornes, claiming to sell the best cakes on the beach; then comes S. Baxfield Fresh Oysters; next appears to be a photographers, but whatever is supplied it costs 2d! At the back of the promenade T. Turner has beach chairs for hire. In front of him is the gaily flag decorated kiosk of H. Norman, selling ice cream, lemonade, etc. Lastly is Lipton's Tea shop. The structure which runs up the cliff to a small platform at the top is the 'Reno' Electric stairway – price one penny. The first proposals for its erection were made in 1901, 'to convey passengers from Lower Promenade to Greensward.' By May, 1902, the Council were complaining about 'Clay being deposited on the beach by the contractors.' The elevator was in use that year: 'It is operated by an electric motor, has a speed of 100 feet per minute, is practically noiseless when running, and has a carrying capacity of three thousand passengers per hour. It has a moving hand rail...' In other words, an early version of to-days Underground elevators. But in June, 1906, the Reno Elevator Co. wrote to the CUDC stating that they were losing money each year and sought permission to remove it. There was financial wrangling for over two years and in the end it would appear that the Reno Co. removed the machinery, but left CUDC with the problem of what to do with the structure. On 3rd February 1909 they resolved that the 'Whole of the Reno Elevator structure be removed and that a sloping path... be constructed.' And that was the end of the short lived Reno Electric Stairway – price 1d.

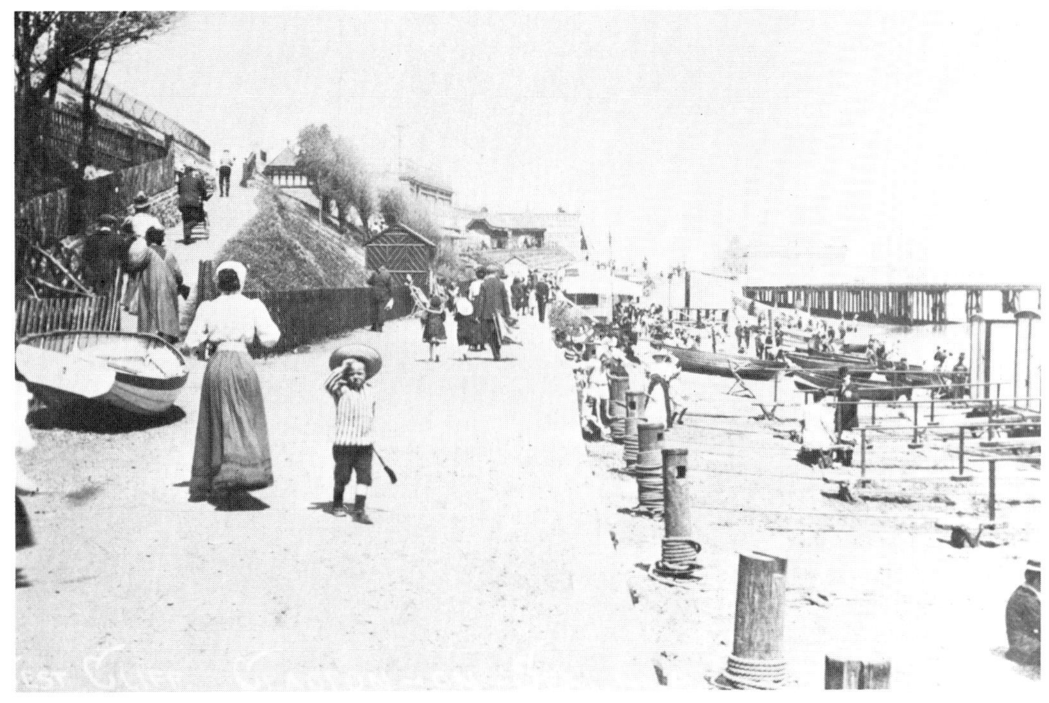

53. This beach scene is of interest because it shows very clearly how the heavy bathing machines were winched back up the beach as the tide came in. The tide is, in fact, still coming in, and many of the hauling ropes can be seen attached to their windlasses. It must have created something of a problem for anyone walking along the beach – the unwary could so easily trip over the ropes. Children of course loved to walk all over the ropes and climb up the windlasses (as two can be seen doing in the photo!) The poor little lad in the centre doesn't look too happy; perhaps he has lost his Mum! The 'Reno' Electric Stairway appears to have been disposed of, which would date this photograph circa 1910.

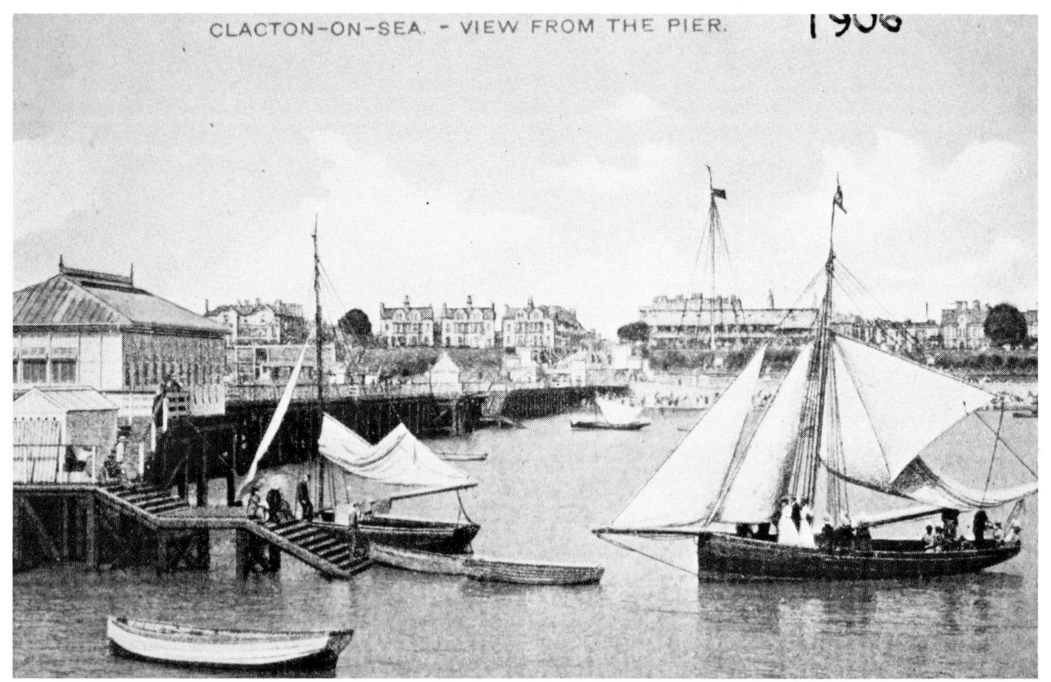

54. CLACTON FROM THE SEA: 1906. A view from the Pier in 1906. A number of sailing craft operated from Clacton in the summer months. Mostly they were the small but extremely handy 'Oyster Smacks' from Mersea and Brightlingsea, who found this a lucrative summer occupation. Amongst their number were 'Gracie' and 'Masonic'. The loose footed, gaff-rigged mains'l shown on the craft approaching the Pier has been 'scandalised', i.e. the peak of the gaff has been lowered and the mains'l cannot hold the wind and so is 'scandalised'. The craft glides up to the Pier steps under her jib and fores'l. It is a calm old day – even the ladies are standing up, by the mast. To get under way again with a fresh batch of passengers, the gaff would be raised, and off would go the smack, expertly handled by the Mersea or Brightlingsea smacksmen. Note the traditional East Coast design of these craft: long bowsprit; flush deck; straight stem; counter stern; gaff-rig with loose footed mains'l. This type of boat was evolved to provide a stable platform for the fishermen to work from. The bowsprit with its jib, and the straight stem were designed to deal with the short choppy seas off our Eastern seaboard.

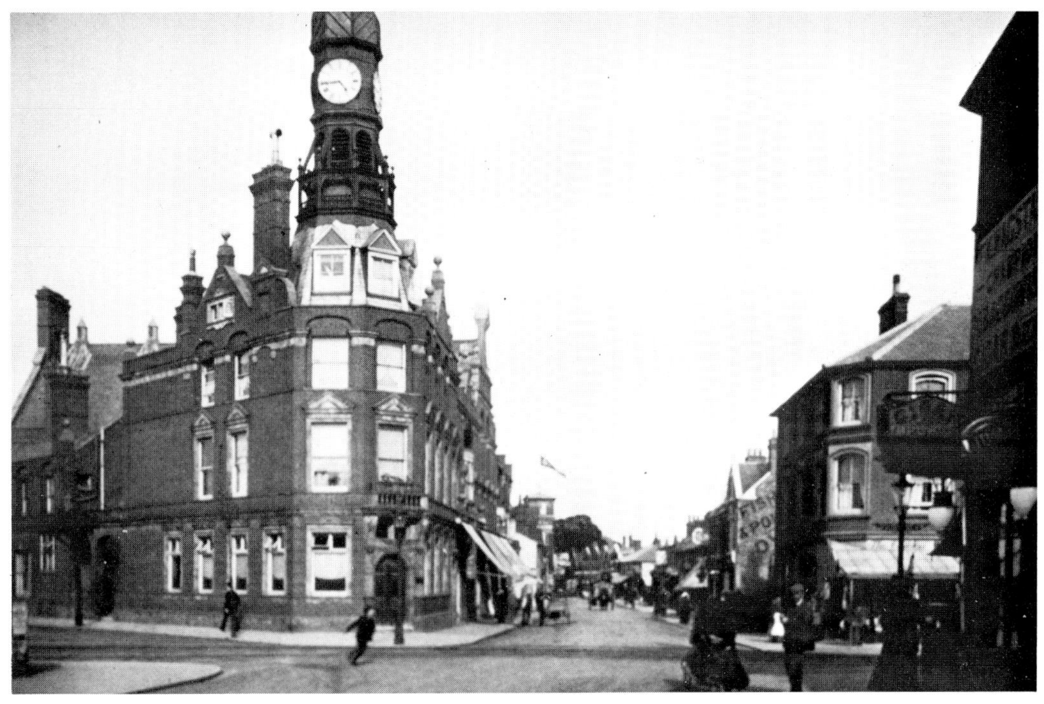

55. THE OLD TOWN HALL BUILDINGS. Looking down Rosemary Road with Station Road running from left to right and High Street going off at an angle on the extreme left. The Town Hall buildings complete with Clock tower were built in 1894 and included Municipal Offices, Barclays Bank (still there) and, on the Rosemary Road side, the Operetta House. The first 'Biograph' animated pictures were shown there in 1905. It was re-opened after the First World War as 'The Tivoli' Cinema, then it became the 'Savoy Theatre' and finally a Bingo Hall. On the extreme right can be seen the Tobacconists, F.W. Wagstaff. In 1941 a German raider dropped bombs which destroyed Wagstaff's corner, and brought down the Clock Tower. Barclays Bank with a smaller Clock tower was rebuilt in 1950, together with a new Wagstaff's corner.

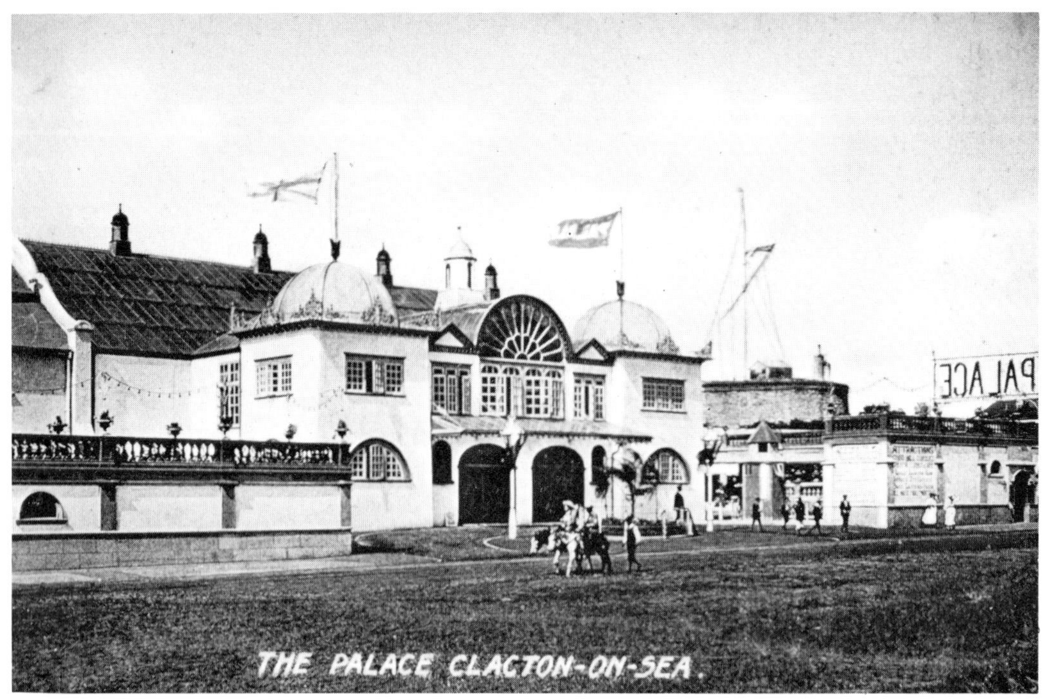

56. THE PALACE BY THE SEA, CLACTON. Billed as 'The great up-to-date attraction built on the sea front at a cost of £50,000, Mr. Henry Ford's Palace by the Sea' was based on the Earls' Court Exhibition of that time. It was opened by G.R. Sims, a popular London journalist and playwright, on Saturday 2nd June, 1906. The Palace had a large galleried theatre, restaurants, and its other attractions included a bandstand, Madeira Promenade, illuminated fish pond, together with fountains lit by electric light. There were the Blue Caves of Capri, a Neapolitan Pergola, Japanese Pagoda, an Old English Home, and various other delights to the eye and senses. It was a marvellous attraction during the season, but it's a long, long time from September round to May, and, like the 'Reno' Electric stairway, it did not pay, and the promoter went bankrupt after a few years. The Palace Theatre survived for many years and then, like many of its kind after the First World War, was turned into a Cinema. It was finally demolished in the mid-1970's.

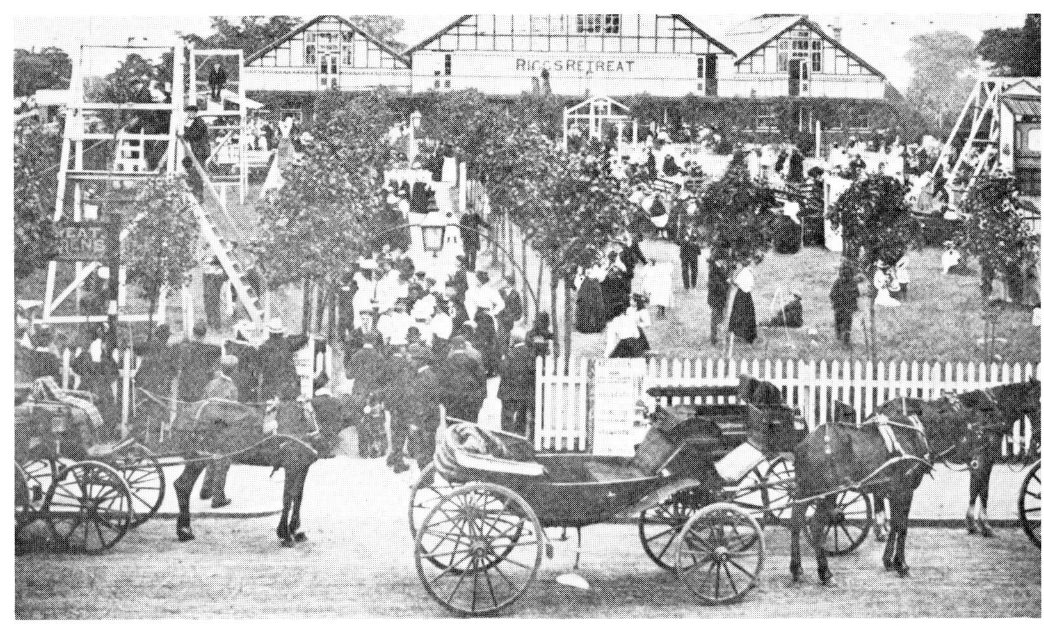

57. RIGGS' RETREAT. *So pleasantly situated, so conveniently arranged and so close to the sea – is not only the centre of attraction for thousands of pleasure seekers in the season, but bids fair to become a splendid winter garden for the residents, with skating rink, dancing platform, and bandstand, all complete* (Clacton Graphic, March 3rd, 1900). Riggs Retreat was opened by John Rigg in 1886 and lay in 3½ acres of ground in Ellis Road. There were four halls, and the largest one, here shown in the centre, could accommodate 1,000 for dinner; the others could take about half that number each. It was also a favourite resort for Sunday School outings. *During the past seven years, on an average 40,000 excursionists have been catered for by Mr. Badger, the proprietor... Those who come once to this place generally pay a return visit, as is shown by the fact that, during the past seven years, 15,000 members and friends of the Hackney Band of Hope have partaken of Mr. Badger's hospitality...* (Clacton Graphic 1902). In this picture, on the left, workmen appear to be erecting two large supports for a high wire walking act. Could this be for the great 'Sylvesto' whose name appears on the bill fixed to the palings in the centre. There is an alfresco meal going on (centre right) and everyone is enjoying themselves, but Riggs Retreat eventually declined in favour as the demands for public entertainment changed and the First World War seems to have put paid to it. Finally its extensive grounds became a Coach Station and Car Park.

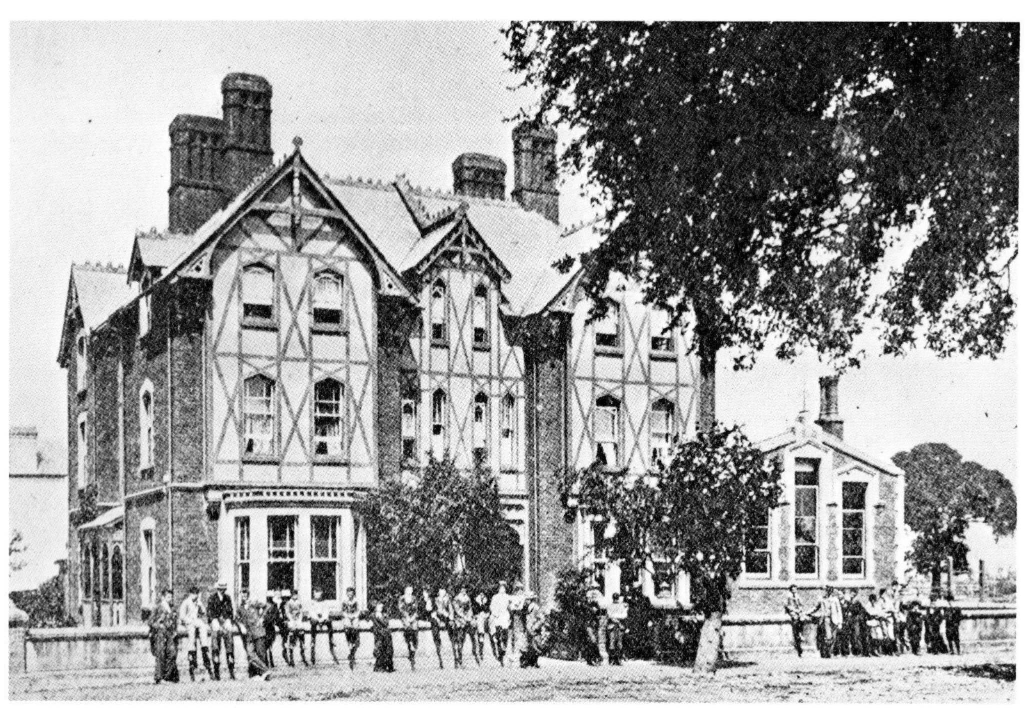

58. ASCHAM COLLEGE. A well known and much loved 'Alma Mater' to many previous generations of Clacton's sons, it was named after Roger Ascham, tutor to Queen Elizabeth I. It was on its grounds that V.J. Woodward played his first games of soccer eventually becoming a star International player for England. A memorial plaque exists in the Post Office building now on the site, it reads: ON THIS SITE EXISTED ASCHAM COLLEGE, 1888-1937. HERE COMMEMORATED BY OLD ASCHAMIANS, 1962.

59. VIVIAN JOHN WOODWARD, ENGLAND INTERNATIONAL FOOTBALLER. A Clacton lad, born 1880, he was educated at Ascham College, Clacton, where he first learnt his skill at football. He went on to play for a Chelmsford Amateur side and, indeed, throughout his playing career he was always an amateur. At the age of twenty he played his first game for Tottenham Hotspur in 1900 and was with 'Spurs' when they gained promotion to the First Division of the Football League in 1909. He then moved to Chelsea and remained with that Club until he finished playing many years later. Woodward played mainly at Centre Forward, but more often than not when chosen for England he was played at Inside Right. He was chosen sixteen times for full International England sides, and was capped sixty times in all for his England appearances in the many Amateur Internationals then played. Undoubtedly his greatest achievement was during the International reported in the 'Clacton Graphic' (3.11.1906) when he played in an England Amateur team against a French International eleven in Paris on Wednesday 1st November 1906. The English Amateur side won 15-0, Vivian J. Woodward scored seven of those goals. He died in 1954.

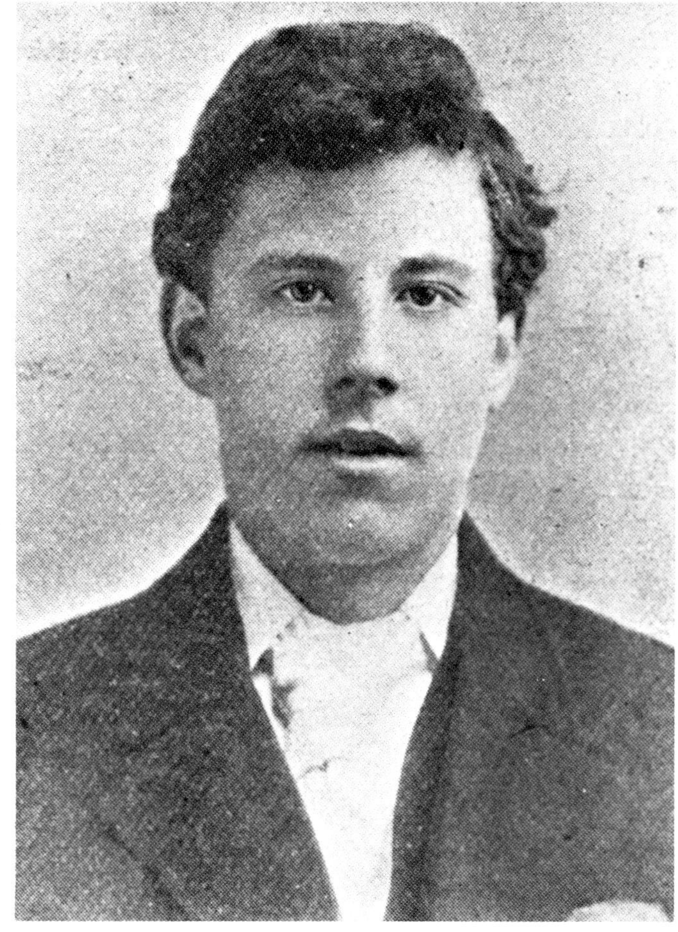

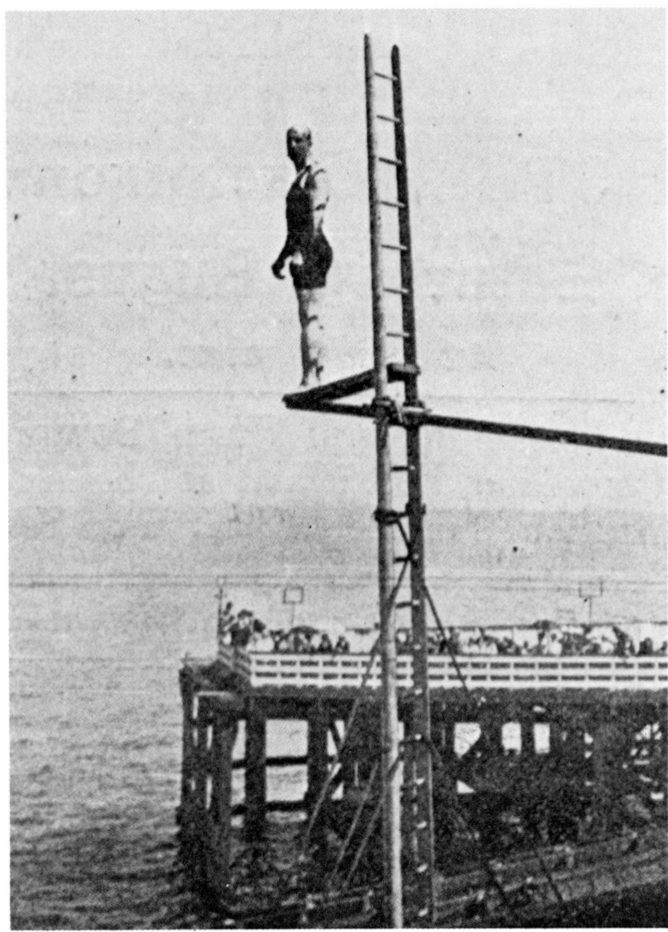

60. 'PROFESSOR' WEBB, HIGH DIVER EXTRAORDINAIRE. 'Professor' Webb thrilled the Summer holiday crowd in the early years of this century with his high diving exhibitions from a soaring extension ladder on the end of the Pier. One of his tricks involved diving with a lighted cigarette, which he would flip into his mouth just before entering the water, to emerge puffing away at the still burning cigarette. He also did a 'Bicycle High Dive' – until one day in 1911 when he plunged straight into a rowing boat that had inadvertently come round the end of the Pier just as he took off. 'Professor' and bike landed on a young lady sitting in the bows. She never knew what hit her until she recovered from severe concussion, in Clacton Cottage Hospital. The badly bruised and shaked 'Professor' also lived to dive another day.

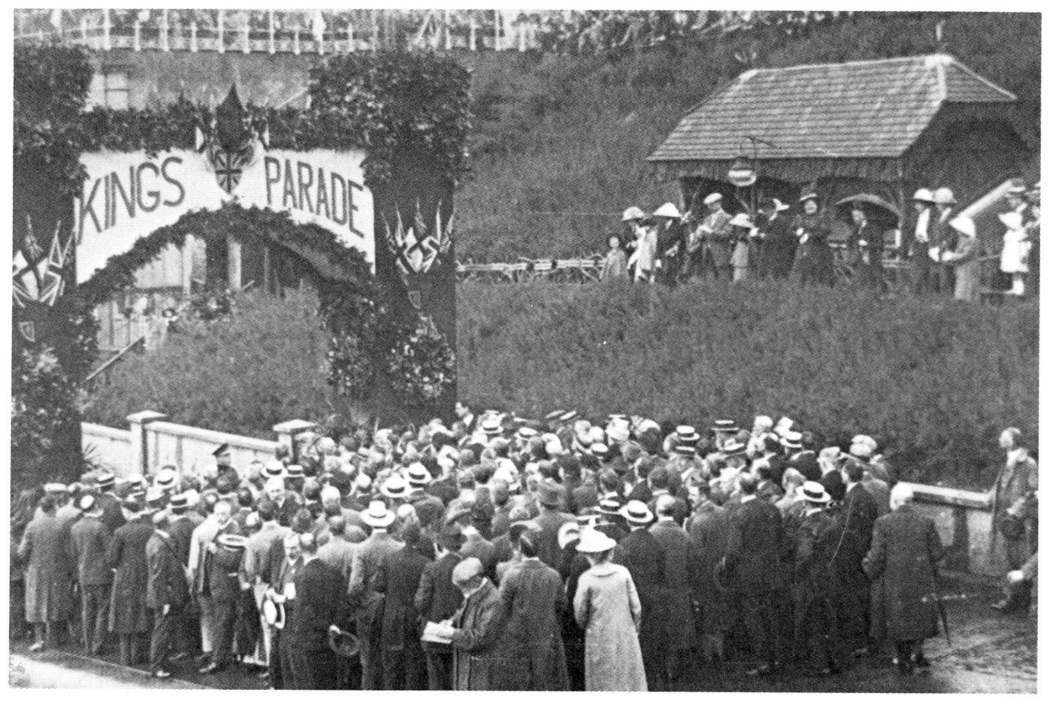

61. KINGS PARADE. The Coronation of King George V took place on 22nd June, 1911 and Clacton Council celebrated it by laying a commemorative stone on the sea defence wall to the West of the Pier entrance and duly naming the lower promenade King's Parade. Nowadays the name refers to a stretch of the coastal road up at Holland-on-Sea at the end of Kings Avenue. It is interesting to record that the next road along was named, in those days, 'Kaisers Grove'. During World War One the 'Kaiser' was dropped. It is now Queensway. The Coronation edition of the 'Clacton Graphic' was printed entirely in purple – and some of the prose reflected the colour. 'The weather', the editor informs us, 'was not of the order now known as Kingly'. To prove it, one lady has her brolly up here (middle, right, in front of shelter).

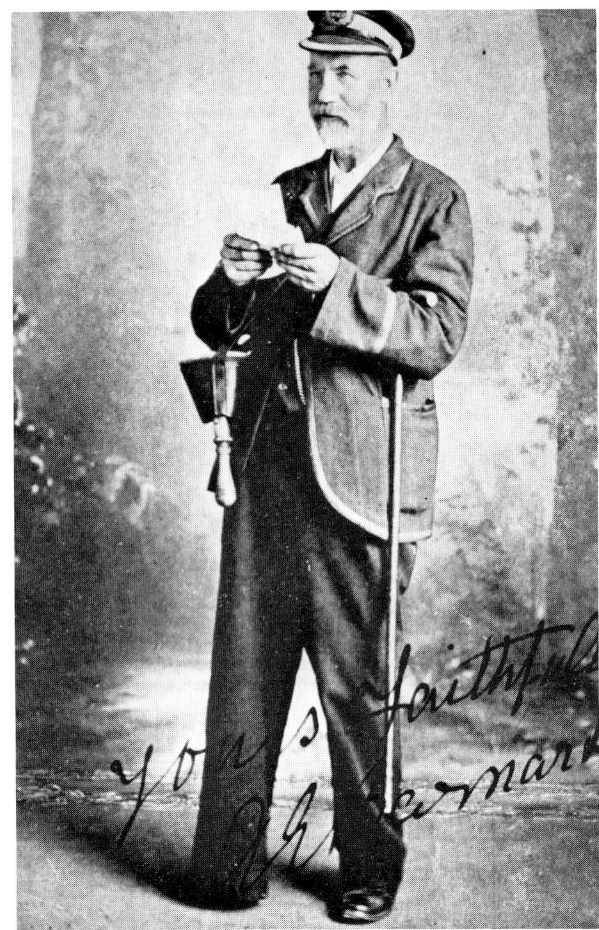

62. 'PEGGY' BARNARD, A.E. TRIALS AND TRIBULATION OF A TOWN CRIER. 'There is no official Town Crier but Mr. Barnard took up the position of his own accord. He will wear the following uniform. Army Regulation Cap with Oak Leaf, Gold Braid, and Town Crier's badge, also blue serge suit. His bell weighs about 3½ lb. Served in Royal Navy and lost his leg as the result of an accident whilst serving.' As can be seen, 'Peggy' indeed did have a 'peg' leg. He has personally autographed this photograph. In 1912, he entered a Town Criers contest being held at Devizes. Other criers taking part included 'Wm. Low, the 'Sussex Treble', The 'Human Megaphone' from Aylesbury, The 'Hallelujah Bellman' of Luton'. Against such formidable opposition 'Peggy' Barnard was unplaced, but returned from Devizes with a 3 lb. tin of Sandow's Cocoa (to build up his voice? – Sandow was a well known strong man of that time); a bottle of Metal Polish, and a silver spoon engraved with the Devizes Coat of Arms. By the way, to prevent the bell from ringing as he walked, it was held upside down as shown by a leather strap attached to his wrist.

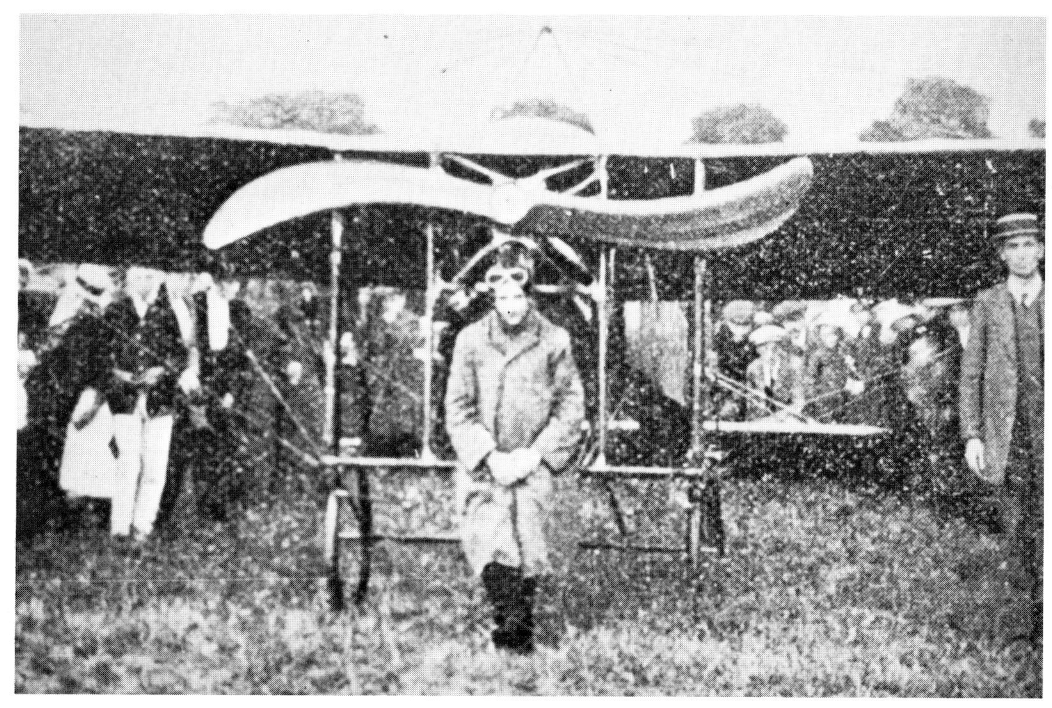

63. THOSE MAGNIFICENT MEN IN THEIR FLYING MACHINES. Monsieur Salmet seated in front of his Bleriot monoplane on August 7th, 1912, in the fields of Mr. Robert Page's Smoaky House Farm, Great Clacton, where he landed after flying the 45 miles from Southend in half an hour equal to 90 m.p.h. Next evening he flew around the town *amid scenes of great enthusiasm, and for an hour provided one of the finest spectacles Clacton has yet gazed upon... The genial and affable young Frenchman threw from his machine bunches of flowers which were eagerly snapped up.* (Glacton Graphic). This was the first flight of an aeroplane over the town.

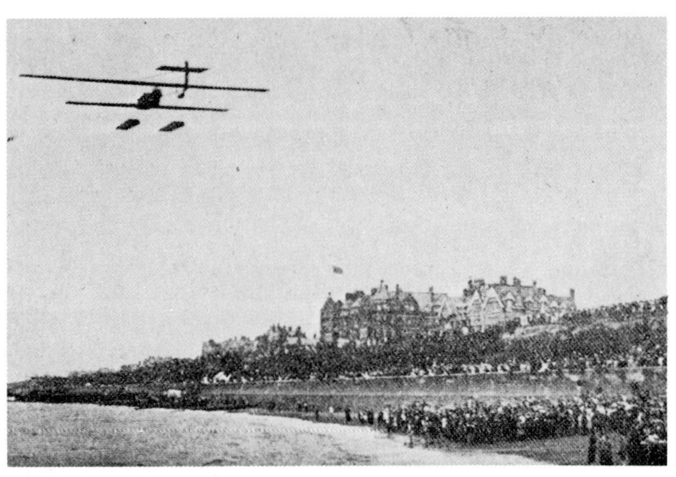

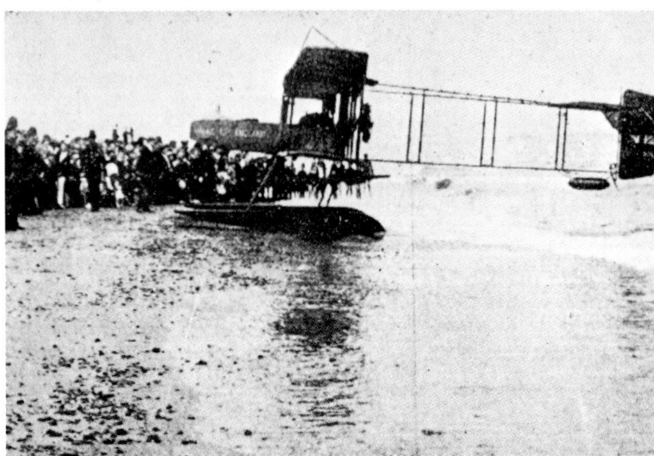

64. 'WAKE UP ENGLAND'. Salmet's flight was followed three weeks later by Claude Grahame-White in his Henri Farman Bi-plane, which had wings of markedly unequal length. The framework was mainly of steel tubing and the 70 h.p. Gnome engine gave it a top speed of 50 m.p.h. There was room for the pilot and two passengers in the nacelle which projected well forward of the wings and the machine could be fitted with either an undercarriage, or floats, as seen here. This 'plane was painted a vivid blue with the struts picked out in gold, while blazoned along each side of the nacelle and under the wings was the slogan 'WAKE UP ENGLAND'. Grahame-White was determined to launch England into the Air age and the seeming lack of public interest led him to go on a barn-storming tour to rouse the nation to the increasing importance of the aeroplane. 'Our people do not realise how backward we are in comparison with other Countries and how our very existence will depend on our having a modern aerial fleet.' (Shades of 1940! – this was 1912.) Lord Northcliffe and his 'Daily Mail' backed the 'Wake Up England' tour. The photos show Grahame-White arriving at Clacton with his wife on Wednesday 28th August, 1912, on the beach just below the Grand Hotel, where they landed shortly after 2 p.m. They were just in time for lunch with Lady Gooch and many friends, after which Claude gave some exhibition flights. *The great crowd was highly amused at the little game the airman played with the passengers on rowing boats. Planing down to within a few feet of them, he would suddenly rise and 'jump' over them, as if playing leapfrog.* (Clacton Graphic). Claude Graham-White was taught to fly by Bleriot, and he was the first Englishman to be granted a Certificate of Proficiency as an aviator. This great pioneer flyer died two days before his eightieth birthday, in 1959.

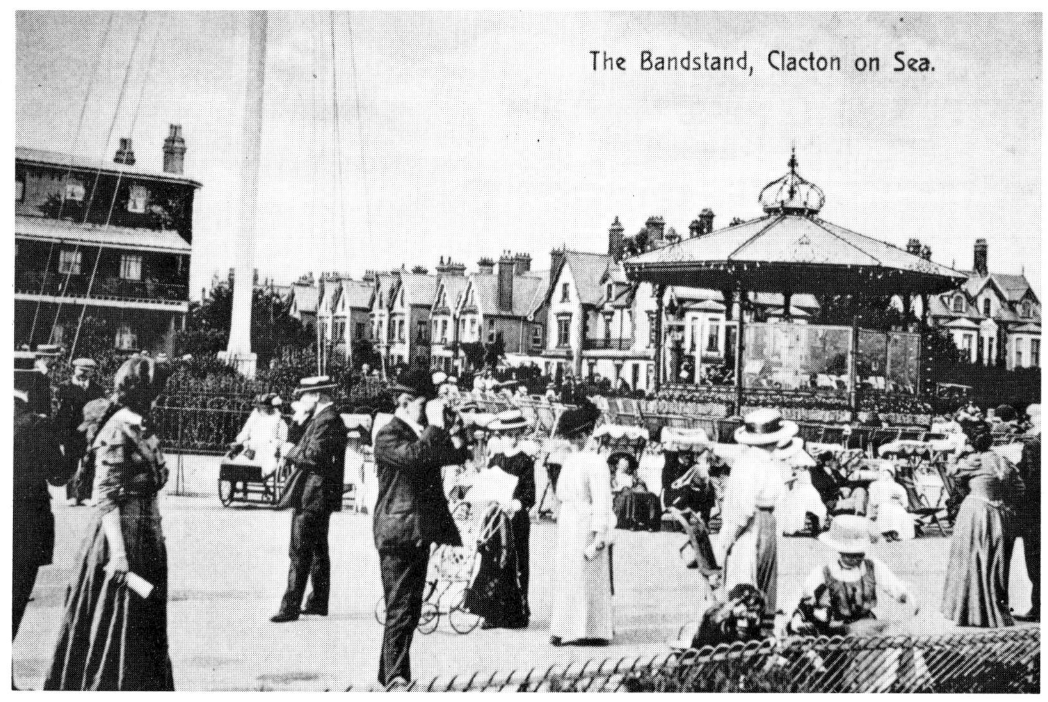

65. THE BANDSTAND. A view of the Bandstand before it was 'sunk'. Concerts by military bands were a regular feature in those days and the bands of many famous regiments performed here. Although it cannot be seen clearly there is a military band playing in this postcard picture which, however, is more valuable as a fashion parade of Edwardian times. Note the lady in white in the centre, accompanied by a Nursery maid, or 'nannie', with a push chair. There is a leisurely atmosphere which is quite at variance to a similar scene to-day. The electric street-lamps to be seen in the next photograph have not yet been erected, nor is the Bandstand decorated with hanging baskets of flowers. The date is about 1906.

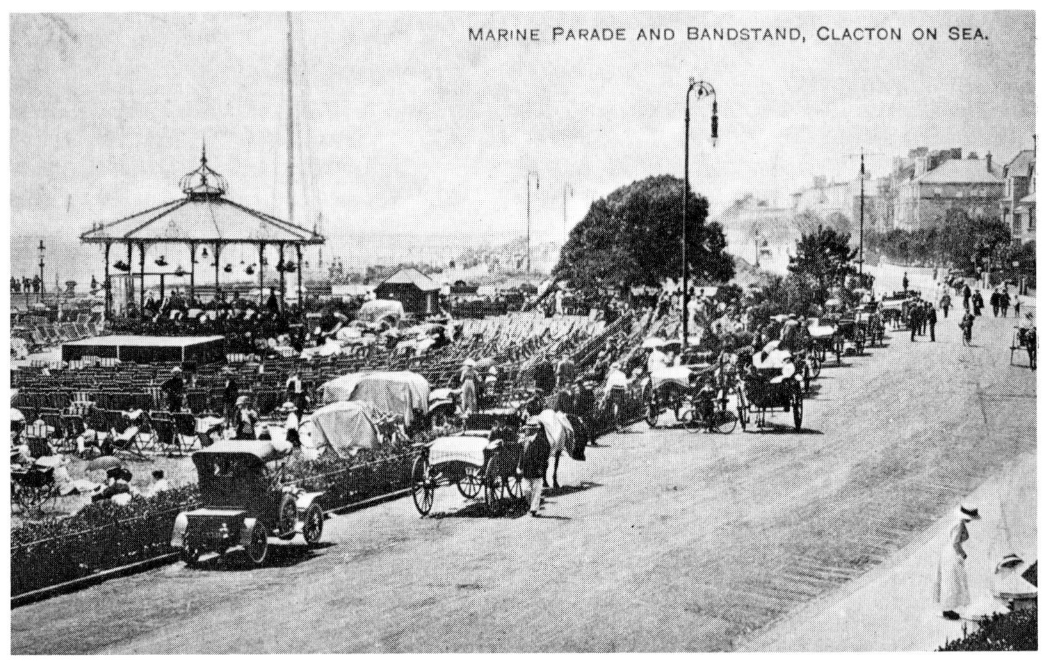

66. THE BANDSTAND (II). A view of Marine Parade and the Bandstand. Electric lighting along Marine Parade was installed in 1912. This postcard was probably taken in the following year. The band of the 2nd Battalion 60th Rifles was playing at Clacton in August of that year. The 'Clacton Graphic' for August 16th, 1913 reported two royal visitors at Clacton, Prince Maurice and Prince Leopold of Battenberg. They were the second and third sons of Princess Beatrice, youngest and favourite daughter of Queen Victoria, and her husband Prince Henry of Battenberg, brother of the famous Admiral and First Sea Lord, Prince Louis. (N.B. The family name was changed during the war to Mountbatten.) The two princes, both in their early twenties: *were seen listening intently to the band of the 2nd Bn. 60th Rifles, we understand that their Royal Highnesses are attached to the Regt.* Just over a year later the younger of the brothers, Prince Maurice, was fighting with his regiment in the British Expeditionary Force and was mortally wounded by German shrapnel in the retreat from Mons. This was the last year that the Bandstand was above ground for in 1914 a large sunken enclosure became its new home. All else is horse-drawn in this postcard, but in the left foreground is an early Motor Car complete with canvas hood, spare wheel, and tool box at the back.

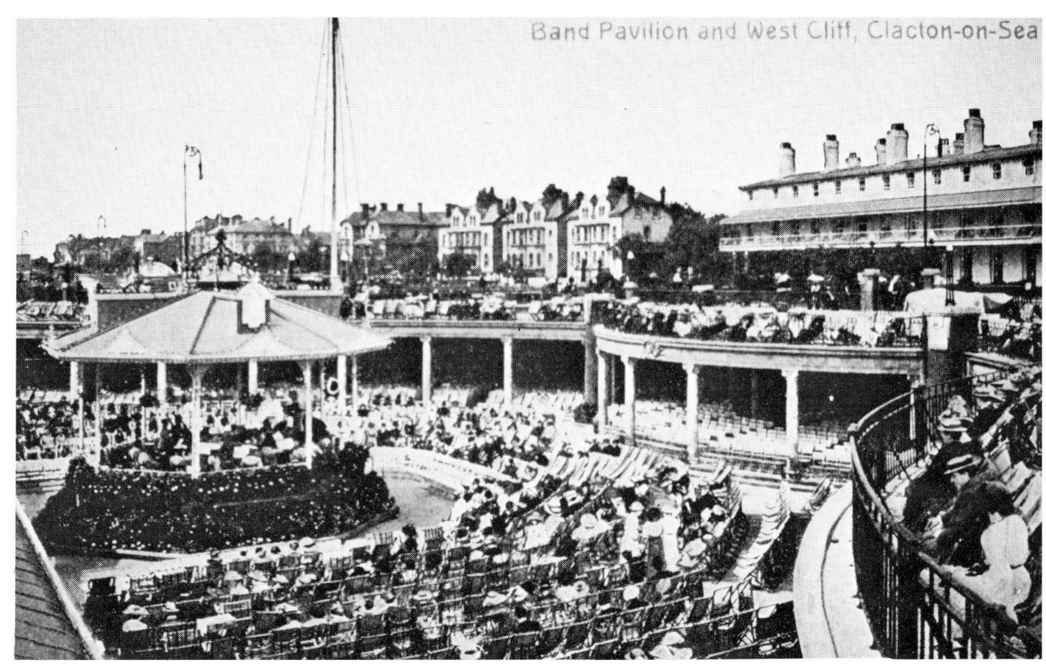

67. THE SUNKEN BANDSTAND AND VENETIAN BRIDGE, 1914. Clacton's Grand Event in the early summer of 1914 was the opening of the new sunken Band Pavilion and 'Rialto' or, as it later became known, 'Venetian' Bridge over Pier Gap. The idea was to make a more attractive feature for the town with the landscaped gap and bridge, and to protect audiences from wind and inclement weather with the sunken band pavilion. 'Originally', said George Gardiner, vice-chairman of the CUDC, 'they put the work out to tender and the lowest was £15,000. They had a very capable surveyor (Daniel J. Bowe). He undertook to do the work for £11,500.' At the opening the Mayor of West Ham congratulated the Council on carrying out the work by direct labour, and, 'in replacing the winkle and eel-pie shops previously down either side of the Pier Gap, with beautiful flower beds and the bridge which stretched from cliff to cliff...' It was all declared open by the Sheriff of the City of London, Alderman Col. J. Humphrey, on Wednesday, 27th May, 1914. The photograph shows the old Bandstand spruced up and re-erected with four little dormers added, and from details shown, including the '850 new white enamelled folding wood and iron chairs under the Verandah', it was taken not long after the opening.

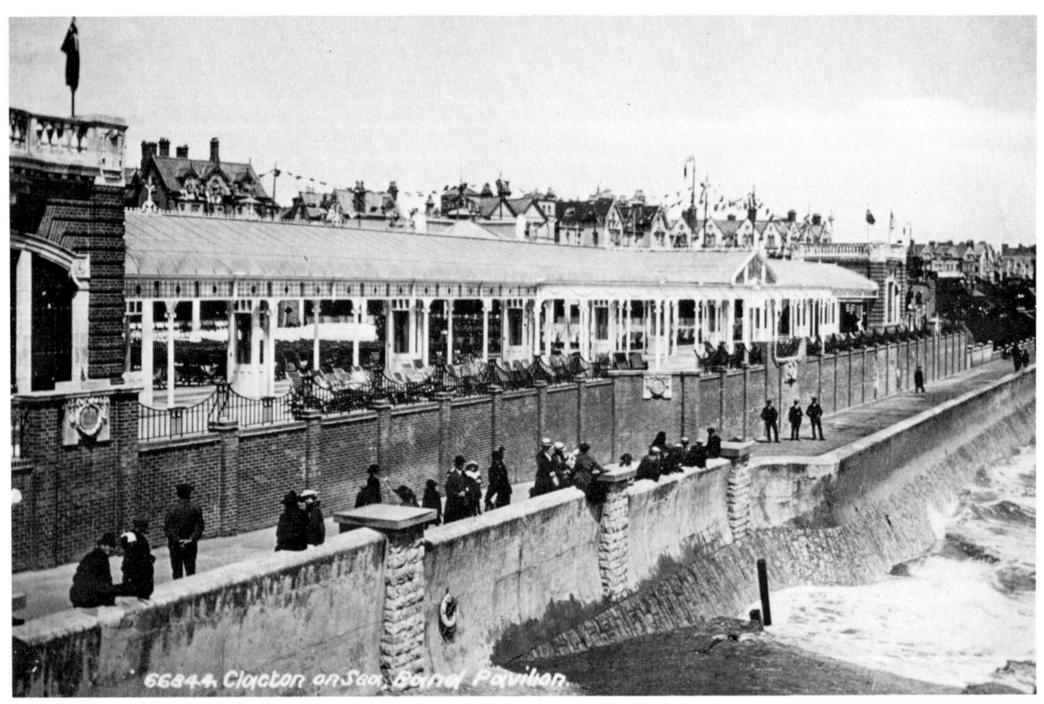

68. This picture shows the seaward side of the Pavilion with its glass doors and extensive roof supported by slender columns.

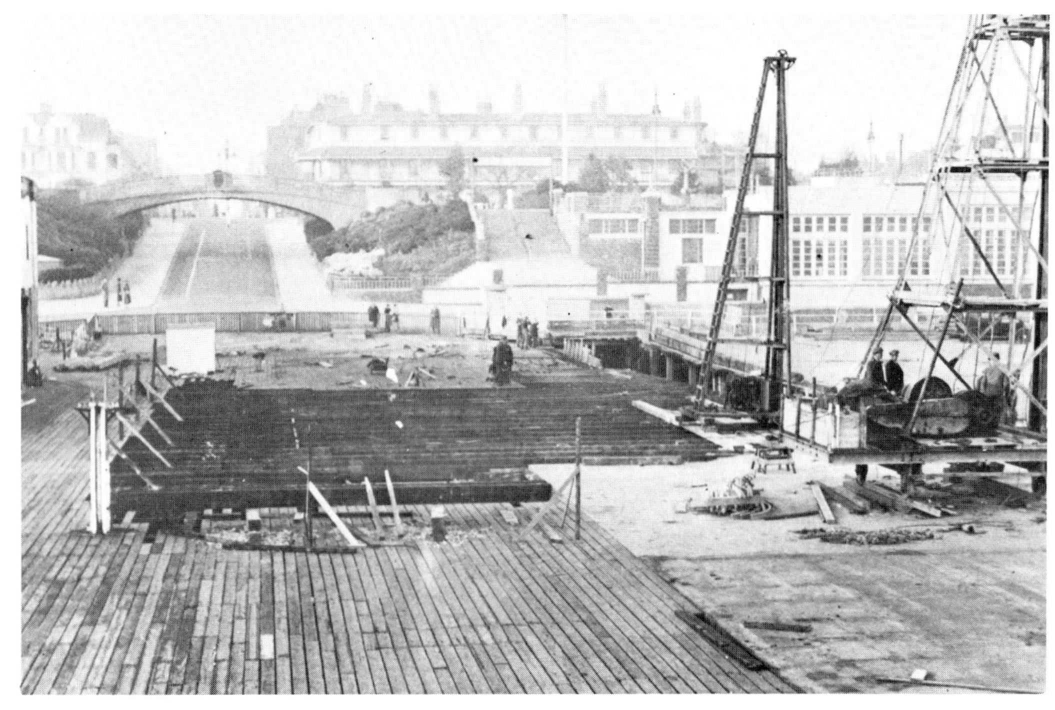

69. Here we see the Venetian Bridge 'stretching from cliff to cliff...'

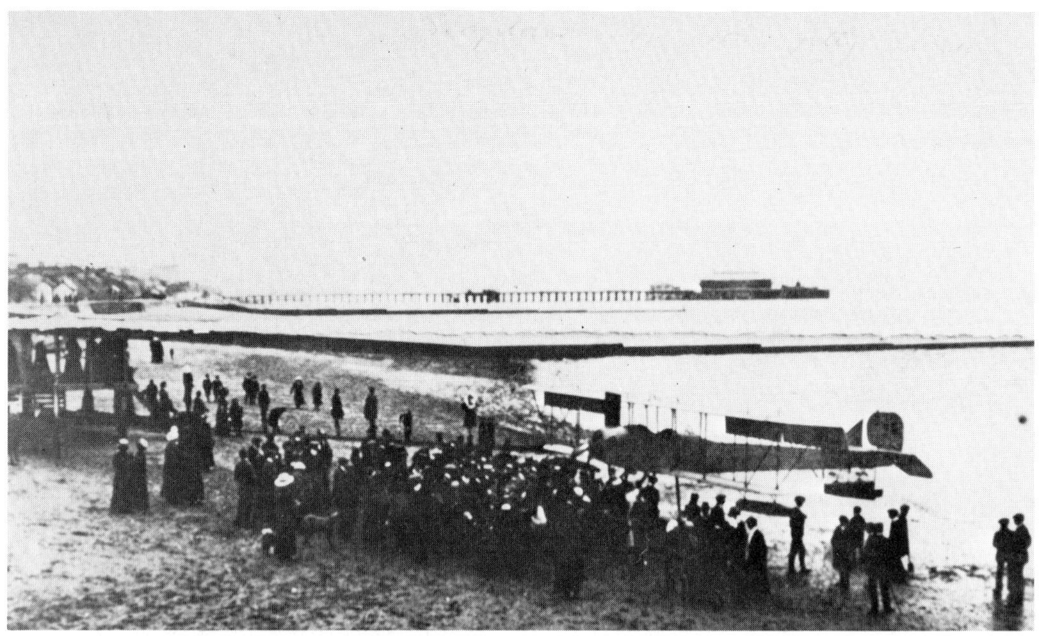

70. MR. CHURCHILL'S 'LOST WEEKEND'. On April 25th, 1914, Winston Churchill, then First Lord of the Admiralty, was all set to join the Admiralty yacht 'Enchantress' for a week-end cruise. Whilst on his way down river to Sheerness he saw a flight of four bi-planes and changed course for the Admiralty Aviation station on the Isle of Grain. There he saw Commander Seddon, who persuaded him to fly with him to see the new Seaplane base at Felixstowe. Winston obviously thought he could make it there and back to join 'Enchantress' by early evening. And so he could have done had things gone according to plan. They set off on board Seaplane No. 79 and all went well until 2 p.m. when the engine began to cough – 'Missing on two cylinders'. Commander Seddon headed for the nearest land, which was Clacton and taxied ashore twixt Pier and Jetty at 2.30 p.m. Winston Churchill was instantly recognised as he came ashore and the news spread like wildfire. After all, a Seaplane landing was, in those days, a rare event: with the celebrated figure of the First Lord of the Admiralty stepping ashore, no wonder most of the town hastened down to the beach. Winston decided refreshment and a cigar were called for and boarded a cab for the Royal Hotel, whilst a replacement seaplane was ordered up from Felixstowe. At 3 p.m. on hearing that it was on its way, he took a cab back to the beach.

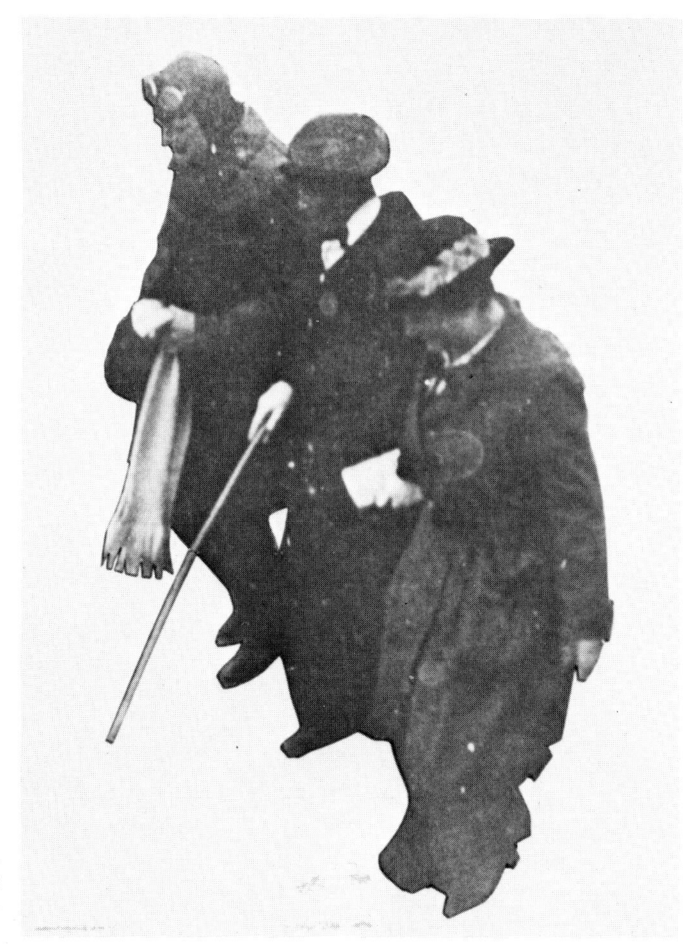

71. ...There he was besieged by autograph hunters, pressmen, photographers – and the local suffragettes led by the redoubtable Mrs. Worts and the Hon. Mrs. Fitzgerald...

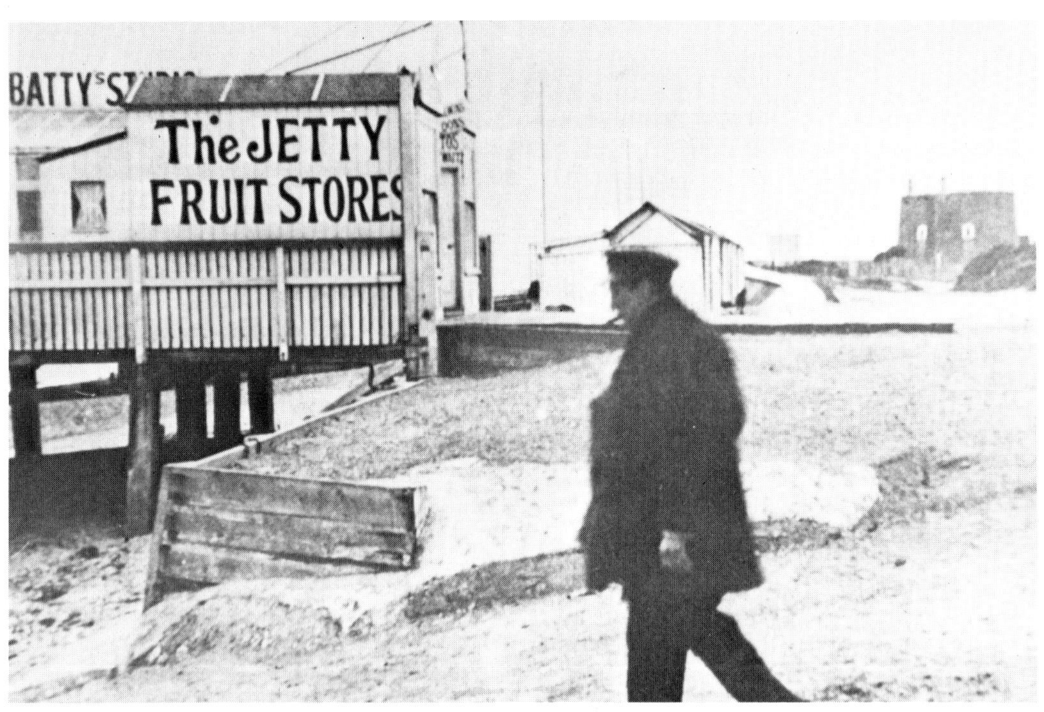

72. ...Things got a little too hot, so Winston retreated onto the Jetty until (the replacement) Seaplane No. 19, arrived after nearly turning back because the Pilot couldn't see No. 79 on the beach because of the crowds...

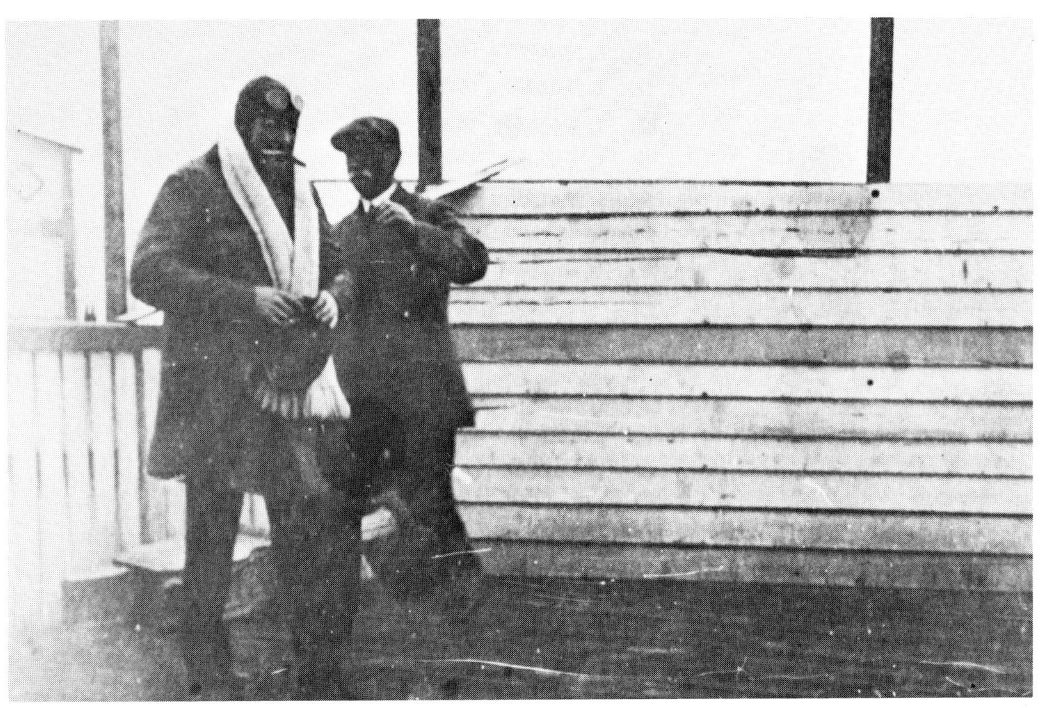

73. ...As he came in, Winston left the Jetty, being helped into his flying coat and helmet by the attendant. Turning to a young photographer who had been dogging his footsteps all afternoon, he said ‘You are a very persistent photographer – can you give me change for a sovereign? This being forthcoming, he generously tipped the attendant with the cryptic remark ‘I like to help those who help me!’

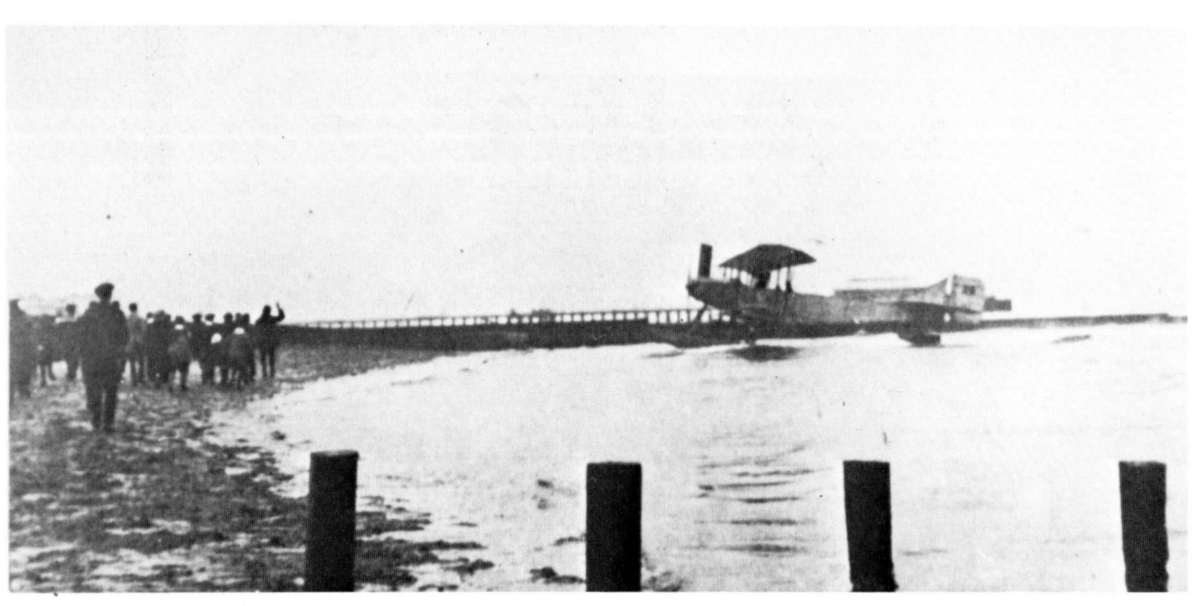

74. ...He left the jetty, smoking a cigar, and went on board No. 19, which took off about 3.30 p.m. amidst female shrieks of 'Votes for Women!'

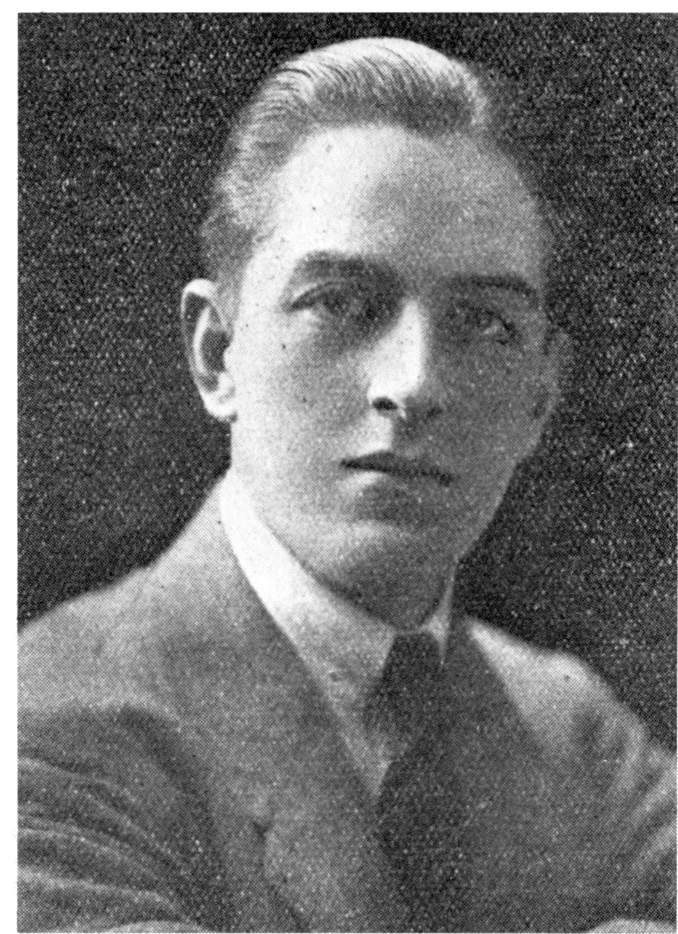

75. 'WIV A LITTLE BIT O' LUCK'. – STANLEY HOLLOWAY. At the very beginning of a long theatrical career, Stanley Holloway was photographed by the 'Clacton Graphic' in their issue dated 21st November 1914 when he was appearing at the 'West Cliff Gardens'. Said the paper *He had already won a warm place in the Tommies' hearts by his stirring renderings of West Country songs...* (The North Devon Hussars were stationed in Clacton at that time.) In later years his most famous role was as Alfred Doolittle in the musical 'My Fair Lady'.

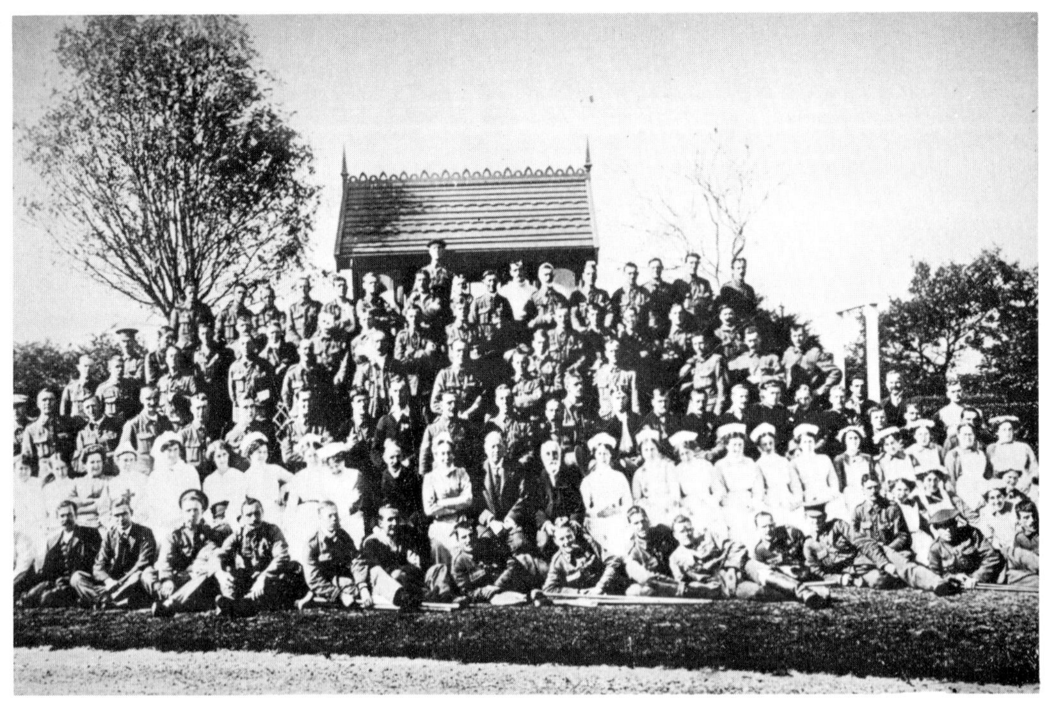

76. A LONG WAY TO TIPPERARY. The first train with wounded soldiers from the front arrived at No. 4 Platform, Clacton Station, at 6.30 p.m. on Sunday, 13th September, 1914. Of the 107, most could walk or limp along to the waiting transport. Seven were stretcher cases. All were taken to the Middlesex Convalescent Home. 'Don't you know me!' hailed a wounded Scot, 'Why, I was the solo piccolo player in the 'Forty-Twa' (Black Watch) on your Bandstand early on in the season. I expected to return in September, but not like this.' Corporal Sladen, flute and piccolo player in the Black Watch Band, had visited Clacton in July and played at the new sunken Band Pavilion. They had been booked for a second week in September, 1914. But the Black Watch was one of the units in the British Expeditionary Force and had taken part in the B.E.F.'s first engagements at Mons on 23rd and Le Cateau on 26th August, 1914. This photograph is a poignant reminder of the end of an era, and is a fitting 'finish' to this collection of photographs of Clacton-on-Sea from its early years up to 1914.